A Shattered Dream

The Cop Who Never Was

Based on a True Story

James E. Crawford

1

A Shattered Dream

First Printing 1992
A Shattered Dream is a revision of the original novel
Officer in Trouble, the Detroit Cop Who Refused to
Play the Games

ISBN -13:9781542368285
ISBN-10:1542368286

PRINTED IN THE UNITED STATES OF AMERICA

A Shattered Dream

Dedication

To my parents, Malvern and Theresa, I thank you for your legacy and lessons of life. To my sisters, Arvis and Joan, as well as my nieces and nephews, Debbie, Bobby, Nancy, Karen, Darrell, Scottie and B.J., your brief visit with life was not always kind. I hope all of you are now at peace. And most recently, to my brother, Alan, and my sister-in-law, Gwen, you all are greatly missed.

Acknowledgements

I offer many thanks to those of you who
through your recollection, suggestions,
and hours of reading and editing made
the completion of this novel a reality. A
special thank you to my editor, Peg
O'Keef, And, where would I have been
without the countless hours of assistance
from my long time friend Esther Luttrell,
who never gave up over the years nor
would she let me give up. Most of all I
I would like to thank my dear wife,
Gertha who read and re-read my drafts
dozens of times.

Law Enforcement
Code of Ethics

As a law enforcement officer, my fundamental duty is to serve mankind, to safeguard lives and property; to protect the innocent against deception, the weak against oppression or intimidation, and the peaceful against violence or disorder; and to respect the Constitutional Rights of all men to liberty, equality and justice.

I will keep my private life unsullied as an example to all; maintain courageous calm in the face of danger, scorn or ridicule; develop self-restraint; and be constantly mindful of the welfare of others. Honest in thought and deed. in both my personal and official life, I will be exemplary in obeying the laws of the land and the regulations of my department.

Whatever I see or hear of a confidential nature or that is confided to me in my official capacity will be kept ever secret unless revelation is necessary in the performance of my duties.

I will never act officiously or permit my personal feelings, prejudices, animosities or friendships to influence my decisions. With no compromise for crime and with relentless prosecution of criminals, I will enforce the law courteously and appropriately without fear or favor, malice or ill will, never employing unnecessary force or violence and never accepting gratuities. I recognize the badge of my office as a symbol of public faith, and I accept it as a public trust to be held so long as I am true to the ethics of the police service. I will constantly strive to achieve these objectives and ideals, dedicating myself before God to my chosen profession... law enforcement.

Foreward

Why Do Police Officers Get Away with Murder? Because We Can

As a veteran, ranking police officer, I see the actions of corrupt police officers as plain arrogance. This arrogance is supported mostly by white citizens, police unions, and protective prosecutors who are obsessed with the notion that if a police officer tells a man, especially a black man, to do something then he damn well better do what he is told. Some jurors explain their justifications for not guilty verdicts for cops as part of that obey code. They feel that if you do not do what the officer tells you to do then you deserve whatever happens to you.

Many officers share this belief as part of their self-imposed code of ethics. "I am a police officer. I carry a badge. I carry a gun. When I tell you to do something, you do it. Period. No questions asked." As long as these officers feel they are covered with that Teflon coating, they will continue to behave as if they are entitled and special, and the abuse will not stop.

The mentality and the system has to change before any real progress is made.

Table of Contents

Introduction

As young children we are often asked, "What do you want to be when you grow up?" The most common answers are a teacher, doctor, lawyer, or a professional athlete. For me it was being a cop. That was my desire for as far back as I could remember. Growing up in the small Midwestern city of Grand Rapids, Michigan in the early forties and fifties, we knew that honesty and integrity were the words of the day, and the phrase "My Word is My Bond" was a fact of life, especially in the Crawford household.

Back then a village really did raise a child, and it was not uncommon to get spanked at school or by an adult neighbor and then get a second spanking when you got home. Parents were not criminally charged for chastising their children like they are today. In fact, spankings were encouraged and they worked.

My first encounter with our school's safety officer only served to solidify my desire to be a cop. When Sergeant Robert Gelderblom stood in front of my fifth grade class dressed in his bright blue uniform, shiny black cross straps, silver and gold badge and gun, I knew right then that one day I would wear that uniform. The thought of a police officer stealing, taking a bribe, falsifying a report, using dope or beating or killing a suspect simply because of the color of their skin never crossed my mind.

However, that is not what I and others are seeing with the police officers of today and that was not what I saw when I joined the department forty-six years ago at age 28. What I saw is contained in the 2015 and 2016 *Department of Justice reports on the Ferguson, Missouri and Baltimore City Police Departments.* And, as you will soon see, these egregious and illegal actions by police officers are learned, accepted, performed, passed on, and protected starting the day they leave the academy. They start out by getting away with the small violations and then build up over the years until an air of invincibility sets it.

What we are witnessing today, and on a frequent basis, the shooting of unarmed black men, did not start yesterday. When I joined the Detroit Police Department we not only had individual officers committing these acts and getting away with it, we had an entire squad doing it and getting away with it. The unit was called S.T.R.E.S.S., an acronym for Stop the Robberies Enjoy Safe Streets.

Unfortunately, nothing has changed in these forty-six years; it is the same music just a different band. The officers of yesteryear got away with it is because the only record of what occurred at the scene was contained in *their* report.

With the proliferation of cell phone cameras, surveillance video, and body cameras, the public is now seeing up close and personal what has been hidden from them for years, officers lying, covering up for one another, and literally getting away with murder.

For a grieving mother, wife, brother or sister, seeing your child, husband or other relative lying dead in the street covered with a blanket, sometimes for hours, is not a pretty sight, but unfortunately it has become a familiar sight.

Detroit's first black mayor kept his campaign promise to abolish S.T.R.E.S.S. and then stoked the coals even more with an Affirmative Action program that turned the Detroit Police Department, its predominantly white, top heavy executive staff, and its front line supervisors, upside down. It was a hard pill for them to swallow, and they fought back hard, spending hundreds of thousands of dollar in legal challenges and losing nearly every case. When I came along and tried to impose my Grand Rapids values, and as a supervisor, my by-the-book enforcement of the rules and regulations, a very agitated and angry bunch of cops let me have it from all directions. To them I was totally out of place and time, a true anachronism and my tenure became a disaster.

My battle with the Detroit Police Department began the day I was sworn in, and never stopped. Somewhere along the line that childhood dream of being a good and honest cop became a nightmare.

Once a Cop – Always a Cop

Chapter One
Laying the Foundation

I am a scrawny ten year old kid with curly black hair, wearing a plaid shirt and baggy corduroy pants held up by suspenders, making a beeline toward my house, running across neighborhood lawns and hopping over hedges as if being chased by a pit bull. Automobiles of the 1950s line both sides of the street, where teen boys are playing football in the middle and young girls are on the sidewalk playing hopscotch. During my mad dash to my house I took time to wave at Ernie Johnson, my 70 year old neighbor, who sits on the porch, rocking back and forth and swatting flies. Ernie glances down at his pocket watch.

"Slow down, Jimmy. You still got three minutes."

Ernie smiles and shakes his head from side to side as I zip past him heading for the house two doors away. Three giant leaps take me from the walkway up four steps and onto the porch of a small, dark-gray, wooden, framed home. I yank open the tattered screen door and race inside passing several pieces of furniture covered with hard plastic before I get to the mantel above the fireplace. I reach up, pull down a badge, pin it to my shirt, and plop down on the linoleum covered floor with my chin resting comfortably in my hands and my elbows planted on the floor. A flip of the switch turns on the black-and-white television where a large police badge with the number 714 pops up on the screen. The narrator begins.

"This is the city, Los Angeles California. I work here, I'm a cop. My name is Friday."

The Dragnet theme song begins to play as a swinging door allows Theresa, a short, forty-seven year old, slightly obese redbone, to enter from the kitchen wearing an apron and with her hands covered with flour.

"Hey."

I don't respond. I am glued to the screen. My mother taps me on the head.

"I need you to run to the store and get a loaf of bread and a quart of milk when this is over."

Before heading back through the swinging doors, she reaches in her apron pocket, pulls out a dollar bill and places it in my hand which is raised above my head. I never take my eyes off the screen. As soon as the final credits roll I flip off the television and run out of the house stuffing the dollar bill into my pants pocket. Bobby and Earl, two oversized teenage bullies, see me running toward them. They step aside as if to let me past, but then Earl sticks out his foot sending me face first onto the ground.

"I'm sorry. Did I hurt you, Officer?"

They both enjoy a boisterous laugh as I defiantly pull myself to my feet. Bobby begins to brush the dirt off my shirt.

When he gets to the badge, he yanks it off and flips it to Earl. The two toss the badge back and forth between them with me leaping high in the air in an attempt to grab it. I am no match for their height. Earl, with a big smile on his face, sticks the badge out in an offering manner and then quickly snatches it back. The brothers laugh and give each other high fives. When Earl sticks the badge out for the second time, I kick him in the shin causing the badge to fall to the ground. I snatch it up and take off down the street with the brothers in hot pursuit. Neither one could match my speed. When I get far enough away, I turn around and flip them the bird.

This memory flashed through my mind as I sat at my desk for the final time in the private office assigned to me at the precinct. I was racking my brain trying to figure out how a career that seemed so promising ended up in disaster. There were those in the upper echelon of the department who saw me as likable, ambitious, and conscientious, a leader who one day may become chief of police.

I have an outgoing personality; I keep a smile on my face and, compromise whenever possible. I am the person who takes the time to pull alongside a motorist to let him or her know that they have no brake lights, hoping he will take extra caution so as not to be struck from behind. I am the guy standing behind the mother in the grocery line who hands her two dollars when she's about to put the diapers back because she has run out of money. Earlier today I noticed that my neighbor, who was at work when his sprinkler system came on, had a broken sprinkler head and water was gushing into the air. I took the time to leave him a note. That's what I do. That's who I am.

I have a sense of commitment to completing a task like no one has ever seen, and I never just take "no" as an answer. I need to know why I am being told no and how I can change it to a "yes." Most of all, I was and still am a man of my word. There is not one single person on the face of this earth today that can say that James Edward Crawford gave his word but did not keep it, a claim very few people can make. I like people, and I like helping people. These are the qualities that define me.

So why am I packing it in? Why am I calling it quits? I had to go back to the beginning. I mean the very beginning. I needed to examine every element and aspect of my life that created a personality and persona that my friends, family and some co-workers loved, but many of my police colleagues hated. I needed to know what role, if any, my living in a small town that was mostly white, and living in a house where expressions of love and affection were practically non-existent, had on my decision making and my semi-fastidious behavior.

Within the police department my constituents either liked me or hated me. There was no in-between. This included all ranks and all races. And in the case of those who did not like me, the feeling was strong, very strong.

I needed to know why my name made the bathroom wall in nearly every precinct in the city and why so many officers could not say my name without adding at least two or three cuss words.

I had partners and bosses who were much tougher than me and worked the same assignments as me, but did not endure half the grief and isolation I experienced. Was there a pattern or turn off that I didn't see, or was I just dealing with a bunch of racist jackasses?

In order to answer these and other questions, I had to take myself all the way back to the fall of 1947 and follow the path, step by step, that brought me to where I am today, sitting in this office contemplating leaving a job I have wanted since age eight. Maybe somewhere along the way or by the end, I will find the answers to these questions.

This will not be your ordinary story of a cop who was treated badly by his department and fellow officers. This will tell how and why the officers did what they did and how it was a learned behavior beginning the day the entered the police academy. And, it may show the pattern that explains what is going on today with so many shootings of unarmed black men by white police officers,

That date in 1947 was the Tuesday following Labor Day and marked the official start of the school year in Grand Rapids. Things were a lot simpler then. My mother took me to the kindergarten class at Henry School, filled out a few papers, and then handed me over to the teacher, Mrs. Scott. That enrollment lasted just about two days. When the office reviewed the paperwork and realized I was only four years old, two months short of the minimum age of five to enter public school, they sent me home. My mother had enrolled nine other siblings before me. She must have known the rule. On November 10th, my fifth birthday, she took me back only to be told that November 1st was the deadline to enroll for that school year and that only transfer students could enter after the school year began. I suspect that she knew that too. I guess her thoughts were the same as mine, "What the hell is a five-year-old going to miss in the first two months of kindergarten? Duck-Duck-Goose? Ring-around-the-Rosie? The Itsy-Bitsy-Spider? Please! Ten months later I re-enrolled as the oldest kid in the class. This bothered me for years to come, especially since I had never failed a grade in my life and because I was almost 19 years old entering my freshman year of college.

I thought I was an ordinary kid. I liked sports, was friendly, smart and I loved the young ladies. My propensity to chase females started very early. At recess while the other boys played touch football, marbles, and softball, I stood near the roll over bars trying to look under the girls dresses to see what color panties they had on, if any. Chasing them around the schoolyard and trying to grab any body part I could get my hands on was one of my favorite pastimes. The girls loved it; the boys called me a sissy.

My first "love" was a girl named Bette Jo. I was eleven; Bette was nine and lived on a farm just outside Grand Rapids. One Sunday morning I was standing on the corner up the street from my house when I saw her walk out of the First AME Church. I couldn't stop staring at her. She was the best looking girl I had seen in my short uneventful life. For some time after that, each Sunday I would get dressed up and stand outside the church hoping to get another look. The thing is her family did not come every Sunday.

Sometimes they didn't come any Sunday at all during the entire month, but I was there nonetheless. After several months of this silliness, I finally got up enough nerve to say something to her. However, her interest was in my best friend, Roy. All the girls showed an interest in him. Roy and I literally lived across the back fence from one another and

19

were best friends from the third grade into late adulthood. He was the best man in my wedding, and I am the godfather of his oldest daughter. That said, Roy and I could not have been more opposite. He was handsome, had an athletic body and curly brown hair. This is not to say that I was ugly and not athletic; it was just that his body looked a hell of a lot better than mine.

Roy had the most toys, a great home, and a ton of clothes. Sometimes he changed clothes twice a day, something unheard of in the mid-1950s. Babe, Roy's godmother, spoiled him rotten with money and anything else he wanted. She was the biggest illegal numbers woman in town until state lotteries came along and ran her and others out of business. When we stopped by to visit her, she just reached into a shoebox full of money and gave him a handful. She didn't even count it. I was jealous as hell. I had a godfather, Ed Jones, the man I was named after, who gave me money but it didn't come close to what Roy received.

Roy was virtually an only child. He did have two brothers but both were nearly 15 years older than him and were from his mother's first marriage. I, on the other hand, was the tenth of twelve, wore "hand me downs", and often wore the same clothes two days in a row. This did not change until my junior year in high school. While the money flowed in Roy's house and life, our family struggled just to make ends meet. My dad had a great job working for the railroad, but he also had 14 mouths to feed and bodies to clothe.

Our family's house left a lot to be desired in terms of cleanliness. Rats and mice could be seen running through the house at all times of the day. They didn't always wait until it was dark to come out, although, that was when we would see the most at one time. I hated going into the kitchen at night. As soon as the light went on, roaches scattered everywhere. When I would open up the cupboard to get something to eat, I'd see cereal and cracker boxes with large holes where the rodents had chomped earlier. And on occasion, I would see them returning to their holes in the wall. I was determined that as an adult, I would never let this be the case in my house. If I ever saw a roach or mouse, I would be on the phone with the exterminator within minutes.

My house is neat and clean most of the time; almost as if no one lived there. My niece asked me if I alphabetized the food in my cupboards.

"Damn, am I that bad?'

She just looked at me and smiled.

When I was a kid, at night we could hear the varmints running through the house non-stop until one of them stumbled into one of the many mouse and rat traps my dad set each night. Emptying these traps in the morning was as routine as combing our hair. I hated it.

From kindergarten through the sixth grade I was a good student getting mostly A's and B's, even in the subjects most of us hated like math and English. Ronnie Snead and I had a fierce competition going for the top spot in the class. Each of us thought he was smarter than the other. After sixth grade I lost interest and I didn't like school very much. As I moved forward to high school and college, that did not change. I always did just enough to get by. If I needed a score of 70 to pass, I may have gotten 71or 72. Ninety was within my range had I chosen to make the extra effort.

My first "police" badge came as the prize in a box of Wheaties. I was a United States Marshal, Wild Bill Hickock. The badges back then were made of heavy metal, not plastic, and looked authentic. I wore the badge as often I could, and made sure everyone saw it. My second badge came when I was voted lieutenant of the school's safety squad.

My efforts to look and act like a cop did not stop with the badge; I had to have more. From a catalog I ordered a siren for my bicycle that hooked onto the side of the front fender. It operated like a small generator. I'd push a button and it flopped onto the tire. The faster I peddled, the louder the siren rang. It could actually be heard two or three houses away if I peddled fast enough. On the other side of the fender I hooked up a piece of cardboard with a clothespin. As the cardboard hit the spokes, it made a sound like a motorcycle. Everyone in my neighborhood including Bobby, Earl, and Ernie Johnson knew what I wanted to be, Jimmy Crawford, the cop!

Whenever Roy and I played cops and robbers in the backyard, I, of course, was always the cop. It is strange how sometimes things one experiences earlier in life predict the future. The course Roy and I followed as kids became an actuality when we became adults.

However, there was one problem that had to be resolved if I was going to become this big, rough and tough cop. That something was me. I was a little light in the ass, about 125 pounds, and I don't think I had ever won a fight in my life. Some of the fights came when people teased me about my appearance. With eleven brothers and sisters you share clothes over the years. People notice, and they tease you about it. One person in particular who decided to tease me was Joe Kemp. Joe was about three years older, a half foot taller and about 30 pounds heavier.

"Jimmy, didn't I see Paul wearing that shirt yesterday?"

Everybody laughed. Paul is my older brother, and, yes, he had worn the same shirt a few days earlier. To make matters worse, the shirt did not fit me. You know I couldn't let that go. I got up in Joe's face. He pushed me away.

The agitators let out a simultaneous "Ooooow" I had to save face, so I did what most of us did back then; I picked up a small stick, put it on my shoulder and dared him to knock it off. If he knocked it off, that meant he wasn't afraid of me and was ready to fight. Customarily, the kid who places the stick is usually the one who does not want to fight. Hell, I knew the answer before I put the stick up there. Joe flipped it off with the tip of his finger.

I took my usual Mulligan and put the stick back on my shoulder again. He knocked it off again. Then I threw the first punch. It never landed. His did. I don't remember much after that. Not only did we get teased about our clothes, we took a lot of hazing about my mother's hue. She was extremely light in color and had silky smooth hair. Her father who I never met, or even saw a picture of, was said to be have been even lighter than she was. I cannot remember how many times I was teased about my "white mama".

This was also a major issue with her and a subject we were not allowed to talk about around her. Rumor and speculation had it that my Canadian born grandfather was indeed a Caucasian.

"My father was not white and I don't want to hear any more about it!" she would say. We kept our mouths shut.

I was three when he died, but several of my older brothers and sisters got to meet him and agreed that if he wasn't white, he was the closest thing to it. My father was the complete opposite and looked more like Wesley Snipes in color. We lived in a two-story house that had only one bathroom and three large bedrooms for the twelve of us. One of the bedrooms had two bunk beds, the others multiple beds.

A large closet and a huge attic provided two more rooms for sleeping.

Both of my parents were excellent cooks, a trait I picked up by watching closely. To this day, I love to cook, and I am pretty good at it. The difference between my mother and dad was that as he cooked he constantly sipped from a pint bottle that had to contain the cheapest bourbon in the entire northern hemisphere, Four Roses. Back then I think you could get damn near a gallon for only a few bucks. Usually by the time the food hit the table he was singing loudly and was pretty wobbly. They were also jokesters, a trait they passed on to all twelve of us.

When it came to spending money, my father was as tight as dick's hat band. He would have to see at least two holes in our shoes and rubber boots before he would consider buying us another pair. Often, snow seeped through the holes and soaked the cardboard we packed in the bottom, which made walking to school in sub-zero temperatures very unpleasant. He was also a stickler when it came to paying his bills on time, a trait I wish I had not picked up because it often left me with only a few dollars in my pocket but usually debt free.

My mother was just the opposite, which sparked many bitter arguments between them about her spending money on us for new clothing and other items we sorely needed. She often sneaked and bought us clothes with money she saved from her home sales of ladies undergarments, and sometimes she charged to my father's credit cards.

When he found out, it sparked another knock-down, drag-out battle, but not in the literal sense. Often after one of these arguments he would go to all of the retail stores and cut off the charge cards. My mother wouldn't find out until she tried to charge our clothes again. That sparked even more arguments. Even as a kid, I did not like what I was seeing and made a special effort not to ask my mother to buy anything that would spark another one of those arguments.

Somewhere around the age of ten I began running errands and going to the store for the "old" people in the neighborhood for a nickel or a dime. I also raked leaves and shoveled snow for 50 cents so I could buy my own candy, Pepsi and whatever else I needed. I enjoyed talking to these folks and listening to their war stories, including the ones from my grandmother Lettie. She was my father's mother and was born in 1874. She died just after my seventeenth birthday at age eighty-five. She had my dad when she was twenty years old.

Although I am basically a very impatient and hyper active person, I learned from these mentors the importance of sticking with a task until it was completed. Just as my parents had, they also pounded into my head the importance of keeping my word.

My high school and college years were the best days of my life under the age of twenty-four. As an athlete, I was one of the best milers in the city, won a ton of blue ribbons, and was in the paper every week during track and cross-country season. I enjoyed the thrill of it all, and for those of you who have never won a race, stepped onto that top tier, had the announcer say your name, give your winning time, and then present you with a blue ribbon, you have no idea what you have missed.

And for the Olympians who have that gold medal placed around their neck as the public address system plays the national anthem, with the whole world watching, that has to be one of the ultimate highs in sports. Despite my athletic accomplishments, I cannot remember ever seeing any of my siblings at any of my races either in high school or college. My mother may have come twice, my dad only once that I can remember.

Being a good athlete was a great chick magnet; only back then we did not call it that. Ironically, what is going on today, almost sixty years later was going on back in the 50's and 60's, white girls chasing after black athletes, especially Roy. Although we were up north and about to enter the sixties, interracial dating was taboo. Those who did it had to sneak out at night. School officials took exception and often notified the white parents, which only made the mixed couples more determined.

Heather, one of Roy's girlfriends, pinched him on his butt as they passed each other in the hallway. He tried to pinch her back but missed ending up with his hand sliding across her behind as two of Heather's friends watched from across the hall.

The two of them walked directly into the main office. A short time later, Heather was told to report to her counselor's office. The counselor, an older white female, was sitting behind her desk.

"Have a seat."

Irritated, and suspicious as to why she was called in, Heather chose to stand.

"Aren't you supposed to be dating Jim Danko?"

"Yes."

"Are you dating anyone else?"

"Excuse me, Mrs. Woodcock, but I really don't see where that is any of your business."

"Don't get sassy with me, young lady."

"Do your parents know that you are also dating one of our Negro athletes?

"Is that what those two little busy bodies told you? And what do you plan to do? Call my parents?"

"It doesn't matter who told me and, yes, I just may call them."

"I can date whomever I want to date. This is the sixties, and this is Michigan, not Mississippi".

"I know this is a fad, dating Negro athletes, but I hope you know that dating him is going to put unnecessary stress on you and will more than likely cause you to lose some of your friends. Here at Central we are committed to looking out for that which is in the best interest of our students and we do not think this is in your best interest. And, as you know, children of bi-racial couples catch it from both sides. That is something for you to think about.

"I can't believe you said that. We're not getting married right now, we're going to wait a few years" said Heather in a sarcastic manner. Mrs. Woodcock turned red.

"Is that all?
"Yes."
"May I go now?"
"Yes. You may leave."

As Heather stormed out of the office, she saw the two girls who snitched on her and flipped them the bird. Heather was still angry the next day when she told Roy and me what happened. She wanted to go back and smack the snot out of the two girls, but we told her to just let it go.

The girls had the cars and usually picked up the guys, or they would meet at the downtown library and then go from there. I wasn't really into it that much. Every girl I had chased so far looked like me in color. However, in order for Heather to get out of the house, she had to leave and come back with one of her girlfriends. While Roy and his Heather went off and did the do in the backseat of her car, the girlfriend, Ruth, tall, thin and blonde, and I sat somewhere until they came back and spent the time on small talk. After a few these episodes I looked at Ruth.

"This shit don't make no sense". We could be doing what they are doing." She agreed.

Roy's parents had a cottage in Idlewild, a small resort town about fifty miles northeast of Grand Rapids. One weekend the four of us concocted some sort of story to get away and spent the entire time shaking the hell out of the sheets. Ruth and I were both virgins and had no idea what we were doing, but it didn't take long to find out. We were both nervous as hell. After we undressed and got under the covers, Ruth looked down at my hardness.

"You...are going to put that in me?"

We both laughed and it was smooth sailing from there on. After chasing the girls all these years, I had finally gotten to the promise land, and it was well worth the wait.

One weekend Ruth's parents left town and you know what happened next. Unfortunately for us her parents came back

27

early. My father had let me use the car and I parked around the corner from her house. As her parents were pulling into the driveway, we grabbed our clothes and headed for the side door, stumbling and fumbling trying to get dressed.

Pure panic had set in. We waited until they pulled all the way into the garage before we made our dash toward freedom. We crossed over the driveway, jumped the fence into the next-door neighbor's yard.

My clothes got caught on the fence and it took me awhile to get them loose. This allowed her parents to get a glimpse of me. We ran to my car, jumped in and I sped away like a mad demon. Ruth's parents thought I was a burglar and called the police. The next day her parents talked about changing the locks and maybe getting an alarm system. Ruth broke down and told them the truth.

Her parents' reactions were mixed. They were happy their house had not been burglarized, but concerned about their daughter having a Negro boyfriend. We had a newly elected black judge in town who was good friends with Ruth's parents. They called him for advice. A few days later her parents had her invite me over. They were cordial, accepting, and told me how much they loved their daughter. They then asked that I not mistreat or hurt her. I don't think they meant in a physical sense. Apparently she told them that she had a lot of feelings for me. About twenty minutes later she and I left the house on our first official date. The black family Ruth's parents had talked to have a son who was one of our classmates.

It didn't take long before the entire student body at Central High knew what had happened. From that point on we did not hide the relationship, but we did not flaunt it either. We did attend a basketball game together where all eyes were on us the whole time. There were several more dates and on one or two occasions she picked me up at my house.

My parents did not comment one way or the other when Ruth showed up. The more we were together, the more the relationship matured. It was no longer just sex; we genuinely cared for one another. We dated until she went away to college and then slowly drifted apart. She was the first and only white girl I ever dated. This is not to say that I did not find many of them attractive and that I was never tempted. Of course I was. I flirted with a few and beyond, but not since my first senior year in college, 51 years ago.

By the time I reached my senior year of high school I was still doing just enough to get that "C" grade. And, I was still entertaining my classmates on a daily basis as the class clown. One day our sociology teacher told us that an exchange student was here from Turkey and she wanted to know if any of us knew anyone who spoke Turkish. I didn't know Turkish was a language. I raised my hand.

Roy and me in our later years

"Crawford, you know someone who speaks Turkish?"
"Yes, I do."
"Who?"

"Me."

"Gobble, gobble, gobble." The class roared.

"Get out!"

"Where do you want me to go?"

"You really don't want to know."

She and I laughed about this at my 50th high school reunion.

A few years prior to this, my sixty-three year old eighth grade science teacher saw the unhealthy path I was traveling down being the class clown and not living up to my full potential as a student. She tried to push me in a different direction. However, she chose to do it in front of the entire class just after I had entertained them. I knew I was in trouble when she addressed me by my first and last name. Her message was slow and direct.

"James Crawford, it is my duty to inform you that at this particular stage in your life, you are on the ragged edge of nothing, and slipping!"

Everyone laughed, including me. I was 14; I had no idea what that meant. In my later years when I did find out, it wasn't so funny. To be on the ragged edge of anything was bad enough, but to be on the ragged edge of nothing and slipping, where the hell could I go? I guess that was her point.

My high school days were coming to an end and college was definitely not in my plans. My heart was still in police work, however, at age 18 I was too young to join the force. But I was ready to get the hell out of Grand Rapids.

My mother relied on me for a lot of things like driving her to the store, downtown, running errands, and she even had me to teach her how to drive. The first and last lesson was a disaster. She hit a tree. Of course we switch seats and I was the one who received a ticket for Careless Driving. I could not let my mother go to jail for driving without a license. Back then they would have arrested her without batting an eyelash. My older brother thought I should not have done that because it would reflect on my driving record. I left that alone. Of my mother's twelve children, only one had gone to college so far and he dropped out after only one year. She pushed me hard to go to college. I knew I could make it through if I put forth the effort, but, I really did not want to go. However, the best laid plans of mice and men often go awry

In the fall of 1961 I enrolled at Grand Rapids Junior College where I continued my athletic career and set two school records before earning my Associate in Arts Degree in General Studies.

GRAND RAPIDS JUNIOR COLLEGE TRACK RECORDS

Event	Name	Year	Mark
100 YARD DASH	MOORE	1932	9.8
220 YARD DASH	MOORE	1933	21.8
440 YARD RUN	SCHROEDER	1932	50.3
880 YARD RUN	MABIN	1959	2:00
MILE RUN	CRAWFORD	1962	4:36
2 MILE RUN	CRAWFORD	1962	10:13.1
220 YARD L.H.	BAKER	1960	23.7
120 YARD H.H.	WOODSTRA	1936	14.7
HIGH JUMP	MOORE	1932	6' 1¼"
BROAD JUMP	BAKER	1960	22' 8"
POLE VAULT	DENHART	1960	13' 6"
DISCUS	PRIEBE	1958	136' 6"
SHOT—16 LB.	PRIEBE	1958	48'8¼"
JAVELIN	PRIEBE	1958	205' 2½"
MILE RELAY	BOOKER POWELL COELING MABIN	1958	3:29.2

FIELD EVENTS

RUNNING EVENTS

In the fall of 1963 I took the next step and enrolled at Central Michigan University. Twelve hours of classes I had taken at Grand Rapids Junior College were not accepted by CMU, which meant I would have to go to summer school or take a butt load of classes each semester in order to graduate on time. It was too early to make that decision.

Me & Dr. Ross, CMU President
at my 50th College Reunion

Once a Cop – Always a Cop

Chapter Two
Adjusting to Being Black

CMU was in the heart of Michigan, about sixty miles north of Grand Rapids. At the time its population was just over 7500 students. We had a grand total of forty-five black students on campus, thirty males and fifteen females. Of the fifteen females, four or five had boyfriends that came up every other weekend, three looked like Whoopie, two looked like Aretha, one was married, and the rest played hard to get.

The school's team name is the Chippewas, "Chips" for short. The white students referred to us as the "chocolate chips". Ferris Institute, about forty-five miles away, offered some relief. It had about eighty or ninety black students. Most of the black students at CMU were from Detroit or New York. While they had grown up listening to the Dells, the Spaniels, Nancy Wilson, Four Tops, Spinners, and doing the funky chicken, I grew up listening to the Everly Brothers, Peter, Paul and Mary, Andy Williams, Frank Sinatra and doing the Bunny Hop, Hokey Pokey, and wearing white socks with a suit and tie. This also set me apart from students at CMU. We did not have a black radio station in Grand Rapids.

However, late at night, we could get a show on the radio called *Randy's Record Shop*. It was out of Gallatin, Tennessee, and 99% of the music they played was by black artists. That's how it was. I wasn't given the opportunity to choose where I was born or raised.

Only three of the eight high schools in Grand Rapids knowingly had black students, the rest had a one hundred percent white student population, and we lived up north! Naturally, I picked up a lot of their habits, their language, mannerisms and slangs. Having mostly white classmates and teammates on the track and cross country teams gave me a lot of exposure to the white culture. Among the black students at CMU I was as out of place as Mitt Romney at a homeless shelter. And, when I moved out of the only house near campus that rented to black students, and moved into a house with all white roommates, to my former roommates I had just grown three shades lighter. The reason I moved was because our house mother was in her late eighties and she had not taken very good care of the house. It was a dump, just like the one I grew up in.

My incessant humor, corny jokes, and running ability helped to smooth the situation, but the black students had definitely labeled me as a hick. The first time I used the term "prick" in front of them they laughed me out of the room. That was almost as bad as using the word "nifty". The only black people who used these two terms are those who hang out with a lot of white folks. This happened in 1963. I think they are still laughing. "Lord, help this poor brother. He has lost his way."

Country as I was, I stilled ended up with one of the best looking ladies on campus, her name was Sylvia, and, yes, she was black. I guess she didn't know any better, kinda like Urkel and Myra. Another shock was that for the first time since the tenth grade, I was not the top runner on the cross country team. In fact, I had to struggle to stay fourth. That was rough. One of our cross-country meets was with our archrival, Western Michigan University. Our team traveled there for a showdown. My old childhood flame from the

AME church, Bette Jo, was attending school there. We were still communicating by telephone every now and then, but we rarely saw each other. We agreed to meet when the race was over. Seeing her again sparked a few flames and we even talked about dating, something we had not actually done over the years. However, Bette was already three steps ahead of me and I was not about to try to catch up with her. She had this burning desire to get married.

"Married? Are you kidding? We're still in college. We haven't lived yet. Why in the world would you want to get married at this age?"

"I just do."

"Well, you're talking to the wrong person."

I was a little upset when I left, and I could tell by the tone of her voice, marriage was definitely on the top of her list and nothing was going to stop her. We didn't communicate much after that visit. A year or so later she got her wish and married a fellow student. It was expected, but I was still a little shocked.

Just look at that form, Wow!

My cross country days at CMU

To help pay my expenses I received a few grants, worked in the student union bussing tables and I cleaned up the field house after athletic events. I paid my entire way through college and never asked anyone for a dime. However, I did receive a few stipends over the years. When I came home for the summer months I painted schools, mopped floors, waited tables, washed traffic signals, and paved streets. One summer I dug graves.

One of the places where I waited tables was at Kent Country Club, a golf course for the upper crust in the Grand Rapids area. One of its infrequent guests was Jerry Ford, later known as President Gerald R. Ford. No one in Grand Rapids called him Congressman; he was just simply Jerry and that's the way he liked it. He was raised one block over and three blocks up from where I was raised.

I saw him a few times over the years. Once was when my mother was having an issue with her Social Security. She had written him a couple of letters, but only got generic responses. One night, Jerry was giving a speech downtown.

That night I parked the car outside the Civic Auditorium where he was appearing. After he finished and walked outside, I approached him.

"My mother is having a problem with her Social Security and she could really use your help."

"Have her call my office."

"She has, and she has written twice. She's right there. (I point to my car) Will you talk to her? It will only take a minute. Please?"

He hesitated momentarily and then walked the fifty feet to the car. A few weeks later, her issue with Social Security was over. I will always remember him for that.

Due to the loss of credits from junior college, and because I didn't bother to go to summer school either year, I did not have the necessary credits to graduate at the end of my senior year.

I was still those same twelve hours short. I also had not declared my minor yet. As I looked over my transcript I saw that I only needed one more history class to declare it as my minor. Guess what? History became my minor although I couldn't remember who we fought in the World War One. I didn't like school any more than I did the day I entered. All I wanted to do was to get through with it as soon as I could. I finished all of my classes at the end of the first semester of my second senior year, 1965. All that was left for me to do was my student teaching.

After the Christmas break I did my student teaching for three months and went back for June graduation. The school I was assigned to do my teaching was Union High School in Grand Rapids. Ironically, one of my former teachers, Miss Skirka from Central High, the one who kicked me out of her typing class, was now teaching at Union. Miss Skirka gave me the only failing grade I ever received at any level, in any school. When she found out I was at Union doing my student

39

teaching she wasted no time getting to my critic teacher to tell him what a jackass I was back in the tenth grade.

Why?

"That was over six years ago, Phyllis. He is now a young man about to go graduate from college and go out and enter the work force, I really don't care what he did back in high school."

Kudos to him!

I knew the very first day we were not going to get along when she introduced herself.

"My name is Miss Skirka and I am very proud of that "Miss".

Who cared? She was also a very religious woman and talked about church and God all the time. You could do that back then. One day the entire class was on edge and there was a lot of chatter going on in the classroom. She yelled at the class.

"Stop all this talking. Do you act this way in church?"

She then went to the Bible. I had had enough.

"Miss Skirka, I came here to learn how to type, not to go to church."

She kicked me out and gave me an "E" for the class. Our grading system went from A-E. She told me that there was absolutely nothing I could do to pass her class and suggested that I spend that hour in study hall working on my other classes. They could also do that too, back then. I did just that.

June 11, 1966 was one of the proudest days in my mother's life. She got to see her tenth child become the first college graduate in the Crawford family. I had made it! Ironically, as much as I disliked school, my degree was in Education.

After graduation I went back to Grand Rapids and worked at several odd jobs, none that required a college degree. One afternoon I received a call from Phillip, a friend I had grown up with. He was living and teaching in Detroit and begged me to get away from country ass Grand Rapids and come to the big city, Dee-troit. He said I would love it. I had heard absolutely nothing positive about Detroit.

My parents and sisters at my graduation

All I ever heard about was people getting shot, robbed on the street, the gangs, break-ins, you name it. With that image etched in my mind I was very apprehensive about moving there. But I had just graduated from college, had a teaching degree, didn't have a real job, and I had gotten a taste of big city life while at CMU. I had to give it a try.

"School will be out in a couple of months. Just come here and sub 'til then and if you don't like it, then move back to Grand Rapids. If you like it, you can stay at my apartment until my lease is up in August. I'm moving out in July".

I nearly scratched the teeter out of my hair just thinking about it. Finally, I threw everything I owned in the trunk and back seat of my car and made that 152 mile drive to Detroit. By late afternoon I arrived at my new apartment, a raggedy

41

building over on Dumbarton Street, in the heart of the ghetto. Phillip greeted me at the front door.

"Where did you park?"

"About a half block down. I couldn't find a place out front."

"Is your stuff in the car?"

"Yeah, it's on the back seat and in the trunk."

"Man, are you crazy? You better get your ass down there and double park out front or you won't have anything to bring upstairs."

"I didn't want to get a ticket."

"Would you rather get a ticket or have all your shit stolen? Besides, they don't write parking tickets in this neighborhood."

I ran back and got my car and doubled parked in front.

"You carry the stuff upstairs and I'll stay and watch the car."

"Watch the car? Are you kidding?"

"Man, just take your stuff upstairs, okay? We'll talk later.

I was already asking myself what the hell have I gotten myself into? After getting settled Phillip and I sat down to talk.

"Look, let me tell you how it is here. Detroit is nothing like Grand Rapids. It's not even close. There are thieves here. They will rob you and they will kill you. You being black them being black don't mean a damn because there ain't nothing here in Detroit but blacks folks. And, whatever you do, don't let anyone into the apartment, especially to use the telephone. They write down your phone number, call back later to see if you're home, and if no one answers, they break in." Back in those days the telephone company supplied the phones and the telephone number was printed on the dial.

"Wait a minute, wait a minute. Hold it. Aren't you the one who told me that I would love it here?"

"You will, you just have to watch your ass."

42

I gave him the Grand Rapids look.

"I'm usually out of here by six thirty. Here's a map to the area schools. You have to call downtown each morning to see where the substitute teaching jobs are. Try to stay in this area. Things went fairly well the next few weeks, and eventually I stopped looking over my shoulder. However, with each passing day I was getting lessons in black history, and the lessons weren't coming from a textbook. When I walked down to the corner store, every person I passed was black. Inside the store, all of the customers were black, the cashiers, store manager, bag boys, everybody was black! When I went back outside, a bus had stopped and was letting passengers off and on. As the door opened, I saw nothing but black faces.

A second bus pulled up right behind the first one; everyone on was also black, including the bus driver. In Grand Rapids, my brother, Alan and two others were the only black bus drivers in the whole city of 100,000 people. Three taxis were parked near the corner with the drivers standing outside. All of them were black. Back home, a guy we called "Red Jessie" and Tony Nelson were the only black cab drivers I had ever seen in my life, and I was twenty-three years old!

As I made my trips back and forth to the corner store, I noticed this good-looking woman who lived in my building, two doors away. She always spoke and smiled, but nothing beyond that. One day when I saw her in the hallway, I decided to break the ice.

"Hey, how ya doing? My name is James."

"I'm Karla. You're the new guy down the hall?"

If I had smiled any longer, my jaws would have locked in place.

"Nice to meet you,, James".

She sashayed down the hall, never looking back. She had

43

to know I was watching. I shook my head from side to side as she entered her apartment. A few days later I was leaving as Karla was coming in.

"Hey, James, what's going on?"

"Oh, not much. I'm about to run over to the store. You need anything?

"No"

"You in a hurry?"

"Not really."

Karla invited me into her apartment. She and I sat and talked a while. I told her about Grand Rapids and me, and she was giving me the lowdown on Detroit but very little about herself. As I was about to leave, she asked me for a favor.

"My phone is out and I need to call my mother. She's been sick lately and I really haven't had the time to get over to see her. Can I use you phone?"

"Sure, no problem."

Fool!

As she talked, she crossed her legs back and forth several times. Each time she crossed them, her skirt seemed to get shorter and shorter. I tried not to stare, but it was no use. I couldn't keep my eyes off her legs or the rest of her body. After talking for a few minutes, I heard her say, "Okay mother, call me right back. Hang on, let me get the number". "James, my mother just got an emergency call and has to get off the line. She's going to call me right back. I think something is wrong with my dad. Would you mind me giving her your phone number?"

I was so mesmerized I never saw it coming. Of course I said yes. As she was leaving she leaned over and gave me a peck on the cheek.

"Thank you."

She must have laughed all the way back to her apartment.

It was the end of the week and Phillip decided to spend the weekend with Corliss. That Saturday afternoon I gathered up all of my dirty clothes and headed for the Laundromat, just around the corner. Karla's apartment was at the front of the building and she could see everyone coming and going. I returned about an hour and a half later and put my key into the door. The door opened without me turning the key. I walked in slowly, looking around to see if anyone was there. I checked the bedroom, living room and dining room. Nothing seemed to be out of order. I put away my clothes and walked into the kitchen where I noticed the refrigerator was tipped forward. When I looked behind it, the milk chute was wide open and I could see into the hallway.

Back in the forties and fifties, milk and other groceries were often delivered to an apartment building and placed in the milk chute. It was nothing more than an eighteen inch by eighteen-inch hole in the wall with a metal-framed box inserted inside. It had two doors. One door opened to the outside hallway and the other to the inside of the apartment. The deliveryman would put the milk or whatever else he delivered into the chute and when you got home you'd open it from inside of your apartment. They eventually did away with them and they were soldered shut from the hallway. Apparently mine wasn't.

When Phillip got home he checked all the rooms again and discovered two suits, a radio, a small television and a toaster were missing. The light in my head came on and I headed straight for Karla's door. She had probably put some small kid through the chute and had him open the apartment door. Of course she did not answer. Phillip later discovered that some of his jewelry was also missing, and several blank checks had been taken from the middle of his checkbook.

I finally caught up with Karla a few days later. She denied having anything to do with the break in and promptly ended our "friendship".

I subbed until the end of the semester when I was offered a contract to teach biology at the city's newest high school,

Kettering. It was only in its second year of existence and didn't even have a senior class yet. Needless to say, I moved off Dumbarton.

Kettering, like many of the schools where I had subbed, was predominantly black, including the principal, assistant principal, most of the teachers and students. The last black teacher I had was when I was in the fourth grade. By this time I had "bulked" up to whopping 150 pounds, but still looked very young for my age. Many thought I was one of the over-age students, and believe me; some of them looked a lot older than me.

Teachers were required to wear a suit and tie back then, which helped a lot. The school was filled with women who looked as good or better than Karla, literally, from top to bottom; this included both faculty and students. Except for the girls I grew up with in Grand Rapids, most of the women I had been looking at the last three years at CMU they were blonde, brunet, skinny, and had a flat chest. That wasn't the case here. OMG, I had never seen so many pretty women, big breasts and big behinds at one time in all my life.

One day I was standing in the hallway, just looking, when one of my co-workers walked up, stood beside me, and whispered in my ear.

"Don't even think about it unless you plan on spending the next fifteen to twenty years in Jackson".

We both laughed and I just shook my head, Oomph. Oomph, Oomph!

One week after assuming my new teaching assignment I experienced another cultural shock when I asked one of my tenth grade students to read aloud from the text book. He stumbled and stammered so bad that I had to finally stop him. It was literally like listening to a five year old trying to read. I had gotten a glimpse of this when I subbed, but it smacked me dead in the face when they began to read aloud in class day after day. It was embarrassing. I asked myself over and

46

over again, how could they have gotten this far. Just before reports cards were due to come out, I was called in by Tony, my department head, to go over my student's grades.

"How's it going, Jimmy?"

"Not so good. Most of my students will be getting either D's or E's."

"We can't have that. Let me see your grade book."

Tony looked over the book and saw that nearly half the students had failed the majority of their tests.

"Are your tests too hard?"

"No. The problem is that the majority of my students can't read the text book. Their spelling is so bad that I now only use true and false and multiple choice questions. And, the day before each test, I go over the actual test with them, and they still fail the test. I can't do any more than that. These are tenth graders."

"You are going to have to find a way to pass a few more. You cannot fail this many students."

"What am I supposed to do, give them a passing grade when they failed all the tests?"

"You're a good teacher, Jimmy. Find a way. This failure rate is unacceptable. Don't forget, you are still a probationary. Make the changes and we'll talk about it again tomorrow."

He got the Grand Rapids look. A couple of my fellow teachers were waiting for me when I came out of Tony's office. They knew what I had just gone through, pure frustration covered my face.

"Did you get the old your-failure-rate-is too-high-lecture?"

"Yeah. How did you know?"

"Welcome to the club. This has been going on for years. Just change a few grades and let it go, buddy. Okay? Don't fight it."

"But—"

"Let it go, Crawford, let it go. Don't make any waves and don't take the job home with you. You'll sleep a lot better at night. Just collect your check and keep your mouth shut."

I headed over to the teacher's lounge where I met up with Nick, Ed, Walt and a few others.

"Hey fellas, what's happening?"

"Not a lot. How are you enjoying your first year?"

"Right now I'm kinda confused. Tony wants me to pass a bunch of students who are flunking most of their tests. They can't even read the textbook!"

"If they try hard, attend classes regularly, and are not discipline problems, just go ahead and pass them. I know that's not how it was in Grand Rapids, but you are in Detroit now, and that's the way it is here."

When it came to passing the under-achieving students, the coaches expected even more. They didn't even want me to take attendance for their athletes. I was very frustrated and was in need of some type of outlet to release the tension. For me it was running. Not only did it win me a lot of blue ribbons and college grants, it also kept me in good shape. For years and years after graduating from CMU, whenever I was uptight or just plain frustrated, I would run, sometimes for several miles. It was very therapeutic and 20 years later it enabled me to prepare for my first and only marathon. .

One afternoon I decided to work out after school. I saw the cross country team jogging around the football field so I joined them. They were running by themselves.

"Where's your coach?"

"Mr. Johnson? He's not here yet. He may get here later."

"May get here?"

"Yeah. Sometimes he doesn't come at all"

I did some checking and found out that none of the physical educations teachers wanted the cross country coaching job. Johnson, the music director, had run cross country in college, about a hundred years ago, and had agreed to coach the team. However, preparing for concerts was apparently more important than coaching. I talked to Johnson and he said he had no problem if I wanted to take over the team.

Walt, who was the athletic director, and the principal, Dr. Sain approved the switch. All of my runners were sophomores and juniors. In Detroit high school was grades 10-12. Fortunately, I inherited the best runner in the entire state of Michigan and built my team around him. I had two others that were exceptionally good as well. I often ran with them during practice and beat the hell out of most of them. I never beat my number one runner. He beat me like I beat the others.

The practices were tough and at the end of each one the runners were exhausted. Just when they thought they were finished, I'd have them do some wind sprints. I would throw a football as far as I could, which wasn't very far, and they would have to run toward it. The one who got there first got to throw it back toward me and was able to take a short rest. It was amazing how much energy they came up with to get that short rest. We would finish with a slow jog around the football field.

The ones I beat couldn't stand it and were determined to beat me by the end of the season. It made for great competition and practices. We finished second in the Eastern Division, losing the championship by only a few points. In the city finals we finished third out of fifteen teams. Not bad for a team without a senior.

Despite my small town mentality and battles over the "pass them anyway" policy, I was able to blend in fairly well with my colleagues. Most of the females I took an interest in were either in a committed relationship, or I just didn't float their boat. Just like I didn't do much for them, most of them didn't do a whole lot for me either. However, that didn't stop them from introducing me to their single girlfriends. I was the new guy on the block. I was single, a teacher, had a new car, and my own place. I was "fresh meat" and was invited to party after party. I had no problem with that whatsoever. I was like a kid in a candy store, and I did not know the meaning of the word no. If the woman offered and she had a pulse and a heartbeat, she was in trouble. I guess I was making up for all of those painful years as a virgin.

Then, one weekend, Barbara, an old girlfriend from Grand Rapids, came to visit me and brought three girlfriends with her. One of them was Lola. Lola caught my eye the minute she walked through the door. She was strikingly good looking with keen facial features and her large rounded breasts stood out firmly from her slender frame. She had a soft smile, and most important, she laughed at my corny ass jokes. I knew already that I was in trouble. She taught third grade.

I invited three of my buddies over for a little get together, but let them know before they got there that Lola was off limits. The chemistry between she and I was immediate. We felt comfortable with each other right from the start. It was like we had known each other for years. There is no way to explain this feeling, but I am certain that everyone over twenty-one has felt it at least once in their life.

Two of the girls slept in my bed while Lola and I slept on the couch nestled together like two spoons in a drawer. The third one slept on the floor. Hot and hard as I was, I didn't touch her. This was a far cry from what I had been doing over the past few months, having one one-night stand after another. There was something special about this woman, and I didn't want to spoil anything by moving in too fast.

After two nights pressed against Lola's back, I suspected that my days of not having a steady girlfriend were about to come to an end. Her second and third trips to Detroit ended basically the same, heavy breathing and touching, but no action. On the fourth trip we didn't talk about it, but both of us knew there was not going to be any holding back this time, especially since I had taken myself off the market. We shook the hell out of those sheets and made up for lost time. Five months later she and I walked down the aisle. That was some shaking!

Lola and me at our wedding

My first full year of teaching had come to an end. I met with my cross country team and set up some practices for the summer. I was determined to win both the Eastside Championship and City Championship in the fall. When I arrived at Kettering for the start of my second year, I had a big smile on my face as I prepared to have my name entered into the record books as the first coach to ever win a championship trophy for the school.

However, when we gathered in the auditorium for orientation, Dr. Sain was missing. He had been transferred to another school and replaced by Mr. Freeman. There were also some new faces in the teaching staff, including a new physical education teacher. When Walt and the other coaches met to talk about their teams and the new school year, naturally I joined them.

"Crawford, why are you here?"

I thought he was joking and began to laugh. It soon became a nervous laugh and the expression on my face underwent a dramatic change when I realized he wasn't joking.

"Why wouldn't I be here?"

All of the coaches looked at each other. It was obvious that something was rotten in Denmark. Several of them began to fidget and look back and forth at each other. Walt then introduced me to Jerry, the newest member of the physical education department.

"Jerry is the new cross-country and track coach."

"What? You're kidding, right?"

"No, I'm not".

"And, whose decision was that?'

"Mine."

"How can he just come in and take my job?"

"In the Detroit Public School system physical education teachers get first choice at the coaching assignments. If none of them want it, as was the case last year, then it is offered to the regular teaching staff. That's the way it is and has always been."

"I worked with these guys all summer and have gotten them into top shape."

"I heard you had and I am grateful, but it's Jerry's team."

"And there is nothing I can do about it?"

"You can check with Freeman. He can overrule me."

I talked to Mr. Freeman who told me that he was not about to break tradition. I called Dr. Sain to get his take on the matter. He agreed with Freeman. Members of my former team also talked to Freeman, but it didn't do a bit of good. Dr. Sain offered me the same coaching job if I transferred over to his school, Northern High. Just as it had been at

Kettering last year, none of the coaches wanted the job at Northern either. After a great first year, I was hooked on coaching and accepted Dr. Sain's offer. I felt no allegiance to Kettering.

The team I inherited at Northern was absolutely horrible. My fastest runner at Northern couldn't have beaten my slowest runner at Kettering. I won one match all season. Jerry and my old team went through the season undefeated and won both the Eastern Division title and City championship in a cakewalk. To add insult to injury, each week we shared the same bus going to and from the meets. Watching them hoist up that trophy on the way home was tough. All of the Kettering team members shook my hand.

My cross country team at Kettering

53

Once a Cop – Always a Cop

Chapter Three
Realizing the Dream

N orthern had a uniformed police officer, Felix, assigned to the school. That was something else I had never seen before, a police officer permanently assigned to a school on a daily basis. Seeing him standing there in his bright blues and polished leather brought back memories of Sergeant Gelderblom; memories that had shifted to the back of my mind when I left home to go to college. I made it a point to talk to Felix as often as I could. We would start out talking about the students, but before long the subject shifted to the police department. It was hard for me to hide my passion for police work. Felix picked up on it right away and made it a point to bring pamphlets and brochures to give to me.

One afternoon, as I was walking through the school's, parking lot, I saw three patrol cars racing down Woodward Avenue one behind the other with their sirens blasting and lights flashing. I walked toward the street to see where they were going. I stood there and watched until they were out of sight. I knew I was in trouble. On my way home I stopped by the recruiting office.

"Hello sir. May I help you?"

"Yeah. I ah, was um—"

"Are you interested in becoming a police officer?"

"It has crossed my mind a few times."

"Come on in, have a seat. You look like a salesman, are you just coming from work?"

"Yes. Actually, I teach school."

"Well, if you join the department, you'll get extra points At promotion time for your college degree."

"Promotion? I haven't even joined yet."

We both laughed.

"Oh, you will. I've seen that look before."

"Really?"

He handed me an application. I was a little hesitant. We talked a little more before I left with the app in my hand and the biggest smile you'll ever see. I was on cloud nine.

"I'm sure I'll see you again, sir."

As I was driving home, I tried to look over some of the material I had been given, but couldn't. I put everything under the driver's seat. During dinner I tried to test the waters.

"I'm about sick of this teaching thing. Passing students who can't even read the textbook or pass a test, and now they took my team, I'm not sure how much longer I can take this. I'm gonna have to find something else to do."

"Like what?"

"I don't know. I'm sure there is something else I can do other than teach."

"Please don't start talking about joining the police force again; we've been through that a dozen times."

I did not say another word.

Despite Lola's opposing my joining the force, I filled out the application anyway and turned it in without telling her. I then took the written and agility tests, had the background check, and underwent the physical examination. I passed them all with flying colors. I wanted to pass everything before telling her. If I hadn't passed, she was never going to know what I had done. As I sat on the couch planning my next move, I received a phone call.

"Mr. Crawford. This is Sergeant Moore from recruiting. I just called to let you know that your oral interview and home visit with your wife is scheduled for this Friday."

I sat straight up.

"Um—um—this Friday?"

"Yes. Is there a problem with that?"

"No. Not really."

"Okay, then we'll see you on Friday. Have a good day."

"Shit!"

I no longer had a choice. I had to tell Lola.

"You did what? I'm due any day now, stressed out as hell, and you drop this on me. How could you?"

Lola stormed out of the room. Things were tense the next few days. The day before the oral and home interviews Lola went into labor with our first child. We spent the entire day at the hospital. The interview never took place. At the end of the day, they sent her home. It was a false alarm.

"You did that on purpose."

"No, I didn't. It is very common for women to go into false labor with their first child."

"Yeah, Right!"

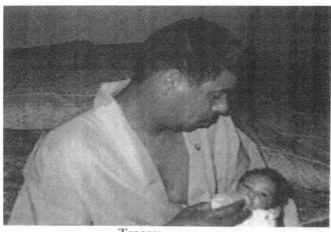

Tracey

57

A few days later Tracey was born. I was happy and very proud to be a new dad, but pissed because my interviewed had been ruined. I didn't bother to reschedule it. Regardless of whether I became a cop or not, I knew my teaching days were numbered.

When the school year ended, I made a few attempts working in the corporate world. One was with Chrysler as a car locator and then a short stint in Labor Relations. Nada! I found myself back at the police recruiting office. I went through the recruiting process again, and again, I hadn't told Lola. I knew I had to find a way to tell her and not have her walk out on me. Lola was that adamant about me not being a cop. As I was sitting in the living room pondering my choices, Sergeant Moore called to let me know that my oral interview had been scheduled at the end of the week. Lola got home about an hour after his call. Immediately, she knew something was up. She said it was written all over my face.

"All right, let's have it. What happened? Who died? What did you break?"

I hesitated.

"I got a call from Sergeant Moore. We have a home interview on Thursday and my oral interview is Friday. If pass them both, I will start the police academy in two weeks."

Lola put down the groceries and slowly sank into her favorite chair.

"I knew this was going to happen one day. I knew it, I knew it, I just knew it. Congratulations, you have your wish."

I told her that I wasn't sorry about joining the force, and I wasn't. I was just sorry I didn't have her blessing. She was angry, she was hurt, and she was upset. I left the house on the pretense I had an errand to run. I wanted her to have some time to herself. I came back a couple hours later. She must have used this time to cry, scream, call her mother, best friend or do whatever she had to do, because she seemed to be in a much better mood. In fact, we had a very enjoyable evening and cracked a few jokes about my new role as "the Man". However, I could still feel how uncomfortable she was with my decision. The next few days were touch and go.

I went to my oral interview not knowing what to expect. I did get a heads up from Officer Felix. He said to give them the answers they want to hear and I'd be okay. The questioning began right away.

"Mr. Crawford, have you and your wife resolved your differences concerning your employment with the Detroit Police Department?"

"Yes, sir, we have."

"Is she going to go into labor again this year?"

"I hope not, she's not pregnant."

"Do you presently, or have you ever used drugs?"

"No, sir, I have never used drugs."

"You are a college graduate, right?"

"Yes, sir, I am."

"You mean to tell me that you never smoked pot or popped pills in the frat house or dorm?"

"Sir, I have never used drugs in my life, anywhere."

"If you caught a friend committing a crime, do you think you could arrest him?"

"Sir, if I were a police officer I would have no choice but to arrest him."

"What about a brother or sister? Would you arrest them?"

"My answer is the same. I wouldn't have a choice."

The two sergeants and one lieutenant bombarded me with questions for nearly thirty minutes, constantly staring me in the face while maintaining stone face appearances of their own. After the questioning stopped, I was asked to step outside. What seemed like an hour later was only a few minutes. I was called back in.

"Before we announce our decision, we are offering you an

opportunity to change any of your answers. If you have lied to us and don't admit it now, we could charge you with making a false police report. Do you understand that?"

Of course that was a bluff, but I did not know that then.

"Yes, sir, and no, I do not wish to change any of my answers."

There was a long pause. They still had not cracked a smile. I didn't know what to think.

"Did I pass?"

"Yes, Mr. Crawford, you passed. Your answers were quite good, however, we do feel a few of them were full of shit. But, you gave us the answers we were looking for. Sergeant Moore will notify you when the next academy class will be starting."

"He already has."

"Do you have any questions?"

"No, sir."

"Congratulations, and welcome aboard."

Those two weeks before starting the academy seemed like two months. Lola and I tried very hard to pretend everything was okay, but it really wasn't. The Sunday night before I was to report for the swearing in, I didn't get any sleep. I constantly tossed and turned, checking the clock every hour. I couldn't wait for 7:00 a.m. to arrive. Lola didn't get much sleep either, but I suspect it was for entirely different reasons. There was no last minute pitch to try to talk me out of reporting to the gymnasium. Lola could see that I was truly happy, and I think she finally realized how much this job really meant to me. The alarm clock never did go off. By 7:30, I had showered, was dressed and ready to go. I tip-toed into Tracey's room, bent over and placed a short kiss on her soft check.

"Wish me luck, sweetheart. Daddy's starting a new job today."

Lola walked me to the door, tightly clutching my arm. We faced each other and embraced. When I stepped back, I could see that her eyes were beginning to fill with tears.

"I know you don't really want this Lola. But I have to work the next twenty- five years of my life and it has to be doing something I truly want to do, and it is not teaching.

I have wanted to be a cop since I was a kid and the thought has never gone away. Maybe one day you'll understand. Please wish me luck. Don't send me out of here on a guilt trip I'm going to have enough problems as it is dealing with the job."

"I wouldn't do that. I love you too much. And I do wish you the best of luck."

"Thank you. That means a lot. We'll talk about it later if you want."

"No, Jimmy, we've talked it to death. There's nothing more to say."

I kissed her, walked out the door and headed for the gymnasium. I was about to realize a moment I had been waiting for nearly twenty years to happen.

I arrived at the gym just before eight, trying not to look anxious. Surprisingly, I was one of the last to come in. As I looked around the room I saw ten to fifteen policemen in uniform. Some wore plain blue shirts, some had blue shirts with chevrons on the sleeve and others wore white shirts with gold bars, silver oak leafs, and silver eagles on their collars. All of the recruits were in civilian clothes. Some of them seemed excited, some extremely nervous, while others acted as if they couldn't care less. And, some of them probably didn't. One of the sergeants yelled,

"Fall in."

Everyone started scrambling into three lines. I had never been in the the military and had no idea what to do. I just followed the rest of the crowd. Next came a booming sound: "A-ten-hut!"

The men dropped their arms straight down, placed them against their legs and stood stiff as a board, facing the front of the gym. Within seconds a tall man wearing a gray suit, white shirt, and a red and white paisley tie entered the room. He walked to the podium and barked out

"At ease."

He removed a piece of paper from his inside jacket pocket, held it in his left hand, and then raised his right hand.

"Ladies and gentlemen, raise your right hand and repeat after me."

He began to read from the paper. "I, state your name, do solemnly swear to—"

He concluded by saying, "congratulations and welcome to the Detroit Police Department." I was so mesmerized that I had no idea what he had said between "do you" and "congratulations". All I could think about was that I was now a Detroit police officer. I did it! I did it! Officially, as sworn police officers we could make arrests, carry our guns, the whole nine yards. However, they did not tell us that nor allow it. The only thing we were given was our badge and handcuffs. I was kinda glad because I had never shot a gun before, except on New Year's Eve. I probably would have ended shooting myself, Lola or Tracey. I wanted to call Lola but knew that would not be a good idea. We congratulated one another, and then all of the paperwork began. I had never filled out so damn many forms in all my life. One of the forms was to join the police union, the Detroit Police Officers Association.

Although I had only been in Detroit a few years, everything I had heard about, read about, saw on television concerning the DPOA was negative. It was hard to come right out and say the union was racist, but many of their policies and decisions clearly favored the white officers over the black officers.

The DPOA often backed political candidates that opposed Affirmative Action, judges who were known to hand out stiff sentences to black defendants, and on several occasions the DPOA was reluctant to provide legal representation to black officers charged with the same crimes as white officer who received legal representation without question.

As is happening today, in most instances they backed their officers no matter what, even when it was abundantly clear that the officer was guilty of a criminal offense or rules violation. They were not about to let one of their own go to jail no matter what. I tried not to sign up, but was told that I really didn't have a choice.

Graduation from the Academy

Once a Cop – Always a Cop

Chapter Four
The Rookie

W e spent the next twelve weeks in the Academy. After graduation I was assigned to the Tenth Precinct or Number 10 as it was called. Number 10 was located on the Westside and rumor had it that only rookies, screw-ups, and those who had been acquitted of felony charges were sent to Number 10. Three others from my class came with me. The first day the four of us clearly looked like raw recruits. Our shirts were crisp and new, and our leather was so shiny you could see yourself in the reflection. We walked around stiff as a board. When one of the other officers said something to us we answered "Yes, Sir", military style, like we had done the past three months in the academy.

The supervisors let the officers have fun for a few hours and then called us aside and reminded us that we were no longer in the Academy and that we held the same rank as those we were addressing as "sir". Three of us were assigned to the afternoon shift and one to midnights. I got afternoons which meant that by the time Lola got home from teaching I was already at work and when I got home she and Tracey were already asleep. It was not the greatest beginning.

Within the boundaries of Number 10 were the headquarters for the Black Panther Party, the Republic of New Africa, and the Nation of Islam. All three groups had been labeled militant and anti-police by the media. Shooting at passing police cars or the precinct station itself by one of the groups, especially on New Year's Eve, was not uncommon. Because of this, every station had to assign officers to guard the outside of the station on every shift. The assignment was called "station security". In the winter it was cold as hell; I mean in the high teens and low twenties with wind blowing. An officer could only go into the station for lunch, to check wastebaskets for explosive devices, and to use the restroom. I peed a lot! After two weeks of this, I asked myself, "You quit teaching to do this?"

Albert was my first partner. He had been on the force six years and seemed to have the propensity of being in the wrong place at the wrong time. He said he had worked with *other* officers who had been busted for pilfering from stores on break and entering investigations, and accepting gratuities from motorists in exchange for not issuing traffic citations. He claimed that he was always the innocent bystander, never taking an active part in any of these activities. He said that he just happened to be with the ones who did. That and his poor work ethics earned him a spot on station security. Albert and I circled the station, blowing our noses and rubbing our cold-ass hands together.

"Well, Crawford, how do you like it so far?"

"It's not quite what I expected. In fact, it's boring as hell."

"You don't know how good you have it my rookie friend. After you're on the street a few years you'll see what I mean. This job is not all it's cracked up to be."

"What do you mean?"

"It's nothing like that shit you see on TV. And as for that pep talk that you get in the academy is concerned "We are not black or white, we are all blue, that is nothing more than a coded message that says that if you turn against one of your fellow officers, your ass is finished." Of course I did not understand that message then and I am sure none of the other rookies did either. Albert went on to say, 'When you get a few years under your belt you'll see what I mean and will feel the same way. These officers out here don't give a damn about you or the people, and, if you cross one of them or don't go along with their lying bullshit, they'll set your ass out to dry so quick it'll make your head spin."

At that time I did not realize what a prophetic statement he had just made. Had I listened closer and heeded his advice, I would not be writing this book today. I just saw him as a bitter cop who had an excuse for everything.

"If you feel that way, why don't you quit?"

"Quit, for what? The pay is good, the work is easy and I have no intention of putting my life on the line for anybody."

"Thanks. That's real comforting to know."

"Hey, that's the way it is. Just come to work, collect your pay and go home. You'll sleep better at night."

Where had I heard that before?

Albert and I had been working together about a month when I came back after having two days off. A glimpse of the duty roster listed him as being suspended.

"What happened to my partner?"

"He's in jail."

"Jail?"

"Read the report."

The report stated that Albert was working Station Security when he entered the Impound Lot and stole a stereo system from one of the cars. Someone saw him putting it in his car. I guess he wasn't so innocent after all.

"Damn, I've only been on the job a few months and already have a crooked cop as a partner!"

Over the next few months I was paired with several new partners. Two of them were also arrested, one for practicing his quick draw in a bar and accidentally shooting a patron, and the other for selling marijuana to an undercover officer. It just so happened that I was on leave each time my partner was arrested. Some of the veteran officers thought that I might have been a plant form Internal Affairs. It was not uncommon for I.A. to use unknown rookies straight from the academy.

I finally got off station security and was "promoted" to walking a beat on Grand River, the busiest street in the precinct. Walking a beat did have some redeeming values. I made a lot of arrests, wrote a lot of tickets, and got out of the cold. I also received my first citation when my partner and I busted a chop shop loaded with stolen cars and parts. The business people loved us.

On the home front things were getting better. I was spoiling the hell out of Tracey, and Lola didn't seem to mind, especially when I got up in the middle of the night to change her diaper or stop her from crying. I had to lay her on my chest each night to get her to go back to sleep. That turned out to be a big mistake. It was a habit that took over a year to break. I took her everywhere I went, including the park and a couple of parties, I bathed her, combed her hair, you name it. We bonded very early. Lola's parents, aunt and grandmother came often from New York and spoiled Tracey even more than I did.

They weren't particularly fond of me, especially after I quit teaching to join the police department. They also felt that Lola could have done better in choosing a mate. I was still a little silly and I would not allow them to continue to shower their only child with expensive gifts and money. I felt that was now my job. The money and gifts became the source of many bitter battles in our marriage. She was an only child, and I was one of twelve. She was raised in the Big Apple, and her parents had money. I was raised in Grand Rapids, and my parents were poor. Adjusting to these differences and my new job was difficult, at best.

After several months walking a beat, I was finally assigned to a patrol car. Both of my partners were white. In Detroit three officers are assigned to a car. If all three are working the same day, the two senior partners work together.

Whenever we responded to a domestic dispute, my senior partner felt it was his duty to lecture the people, mostly black, about their values and how to raise their children. His advice was not well received by the people or me. I was nearing the end of my first year and would be going from being a probationary officer to the real thing. That only meant that the department could no longer fire me without cause, and that I could now tell my senior partner to kiss my black ass without fear of reprisals.

Two weeks out, some of us got together at my house to plan our confirmation party. Lola's mother had just had surgery. Lola and Tracey went to New York to be with her. Harold, Fred, Robert and I, along with a few other members from our graduating class, 70K, sat around exchanging war stories and deciding where and when to have the party. At twenty-two, Fred was the youngest in the bunch. However, he had been with the department the longest, having spent three years as a cadet. A little more than twenty-four hours after the gathering, I got a gut-wrenching phone call at three in the morning. A loud, screaming, and sobbing voice came on the phone.

"Crawford, Crawford, Freddie is dead."

"What? Who is this?"

"This is Dorothy. Fred Hunter is dead."

Dorothy was Harold's wife. My heart began to pound. I sat straight up in the bed.

"What are you talking about? What happened?"

"Some woman shot him."

She just kept screaming over the phone.

"Dee Dee is at the hospital with Theresa."

I was finally able to calm Dorothy down and find out what happened. Fred and his partner, Ron, working in plainclothes, were investigating a man who had just passed a gun to his female companion. When they identified themselves as police officers, the couple began running down the street.

They ran up a long flight of steps leading to an apartment. It was pitch black at the top.

However, the streetlights made Fred visible to them at the bottom of the stairs. They fired one shot. The bullet hit his heart. He died instantly. In those days vests weren't mandatory and were seldom used. Stunned cannot come close to describing what I felt as I sat there in the bed. I was shaking like a leaf. I rushed downstairs and out the door, but not before stopping to look at the chair Fred had been sitting in just twenty-four hours ago. I saw him and that infectious smile he always had on his face. All the way downtown I was hoping it was a mistake. I hoped that someone had gotten the information wrong, that Fred was still alive.

When I arrived at the homicide section, Harold, Ron, Robert and several others were in the report room. The mood was glum and there wasn't a dry eye in the place. I walked over to Ron and looked over his shoulder. The report he was typing was titled, "Fatal Shooting of a Police Officer." My heart sunk even further. Actually seeing it on paper had a finality that wasn't present on the way downtown. Talking to each other eased things a little, but the pain was overwhelming. An hour later I went back home. Up to this point I had not shed a tear. Later that morning I went to see Theresa, Fred's widow. Even that sounded strange, Fred's widow. A few hours earlier she was his wife.

The next few days leading up to the funeral were very emotionally packed. Harold, Robert and I were assigned out from our regular duties to assist Fred's family. It was a department tradition. After leaving Fred's place each night I had to come home to an empty house. That was not easy. Lola had been gone over a week and her father, aunt and grandmother were all there with her mother. I told her what happened to Fred and asked her to come home. She said no. She was going to stay in New York awhile longer. Before she left we had a very bitter argument concerning a revelation from my past. It was something that happened before we ever met. She was justified in being angry with me, but I did not think it justified her not coming back home to be with me in my time of need.

Slain police officers are given military funerals that tend to be very emotional, especially the twenty one-gun salute. Fred's was no different. The day of his funeral officers began to line up as early as nine o'clock in the morning.

As is tradition, officers attended from departments all across the state and several from other states. As the mile long motorcade of police cars with red and blue flashing lights, officers on motorcycles, and dignitaries in city owned cars, slowly rolled down the streets of Detroit toward the cemetery, people quickly line up along both sides, many saluting at the hearse as it passed by. That was rough on all of us who were sitting inside the family car. Dignitaries such as the mayor, city councilmen, and state senators attended. Fred was buried in full uniform. I, along with five other classmates, served as pallbearers.

At the cemetery, the flag, that had been draped over the coffin was folded and presented to Theresa. It is a sight one never forgets, nor gets used to seeing. I thought I had handled myself exceptionally well up to the day of the funeral. I seemed to be in complete control of my emotions. I still hadn't shed a tear and began to wonder if the twelve short months on the job and dealing with hard-core thugs had made me so hard and callous that I couldn't shed a tear for my fallen brother and good friend.

As the other five pallbearers and I stood next to the coffin inside the church, family, friends, and the other fifty-six members of class 70K filed past. Most of them were in tears. It was getting to be too much, even for me. I could feel the tears slowly beginning to roll down my face. Following the twenty-one-gun salute at the cemetery and Theresa's emotional outburst, I totally lost it. I ran up the hill to a secluded section of the cemetery and just opened up. Harold came up and put his arm around my shoulder.

"Let it out, man. Let it out. You've been holding that shit in all week. Ain't a damn thing wrong with a man crying, I've certainly done my share this week."

"You okay now?" Robert asked.

"Yeah, I'm okay." It felt good just to let it all go.

An officer dying in the line of duty is a fact of life that never drifts far from the thoughts of any man or woman who puts on a uniform. Each death challenges his or her commitment to the profession. Experiencing the loss of a fellow officer is difficult in itself, but having personally known and worked with the officer makes the death even more traumatic. One minute you are laughing and joking in the locker room; the next minute, he is lying dead on the street. Walking past his locker, and then through the precinct parking lot at the end of the shift, seeing his parked car, and knowing that he will never get in it again, shatters the very soul.

But, as cops we all know this is a possibility when we sign on that dotted line. We also know that this will only be a temporary crack in our armor and will repair itself over time. We will be extremely cautious for a while, and then gradually we drift back into our world of invincibility, until one of us is struck down again. Why? Because that's what cops do. Two weeks after the funeral, an impromptu confirmation party was held in Fred's honor.

By early fall a mass recruitment drive had begun. This time the goal was to hire a large number of college students, especially black college students. Because I was one of the few black officers on the force with a college degree, I was handpicked to help in the drive. I didn't want the job and fought hard not to leave Number 10. The command officers encouraged me to take the assignment and assured me that it could help me in future promotions. I balked as long as I could before finally succumbing to the pressure. I was transferred to the recruiting section. My new partner at Recruiting was Vivian. Vivian was a few years older but had never worked the streets because department policy did not allow it.

She was known as miss "Goody Two Shoes." And, with my reputation, it was thought we would make an excellent team. They were right. Over the next two months Vivian and I conducted recruitment drives at colleges throughout the city and some out of state. The response from the college students was less than enthusiastic. Just think about it. Why in the hell would someone who just spent four years and thousands of dollars to obtain a college degree give that up to be a police officer on the streets of Detroit, unless they were like me and wanted to be a cop since childhood? This assignment only served to strengthen my argument that I belonged on the street and not on some college campus.

One night after another fruitless day of recruiting, Vivian invited me to go with her to the monthly meeting of our union, the DPOA. I had little desire to attend.

"Look, you're paying dues each month. They've got free booze and food, so get up off your dead ass and go. Besides, from what I hear, it's supposed to be a special meeting tonight. I'll pick you up at six."

The meeting was called to order. After dealing with the preliminaries, the main topic of the night came up; pay raises. The union president and lawyer had put together a plan they thought would put pressure on the city to give us the raise. They felt that if we slowed down service and made the citizens angry, the chief and other city officials would give in to the union demands. According to the plan, we were to take our time getting to our radio runs by driving cautiously. We were to take extra time filling out reports and double check their accuracy, and we were to spend more time talking to the victims about the crime and possible ways to prevent crime.

73

We hadn't been doing this. I thought the plan was stupid. The union plan was to begin right away.

Police officers, like many other public employees, are not allowed to go on strike. I didn't plan on participating because I knew it only was going to hurt one segment of the community. I agonized over it for two days before making a bold and controversial move. I had a friend named Mike Graham who was a reporter at the *Detroit Free Press*. I gave Mike a call and told him about the plan. Yeah, that was dumb. The next day the story appeared on page one, my picture and all.

By the end of the day I had been interviewed by all three of the local networks. The interviews were aired on the six o'clock news. That night I received call after call at home. Some were positive, but most of them were negative and peppered with threats and warnings to me to be careful and watch my back. The reaction was widespread and for the next few days the phone line at the recruiting section rang off the hook. Most of the calls were from disgruntled police officers threatening me with physical harm. The DPOA plan had been exposed and was now inoperable. It had been blown out of the water. Had I done more harm than good? I wasn't sure. This may have been one of those times when I was the one who created my own grief.

Much to my surprise I received as much flak from the black officers as I did from the white ones. They accused me of ruining their slim chances of promotion. My boss at recruiting warned me to watch my ass.

"These guys don't play. You're messing with their livelihood, and they'll hurt you."

I did not have a good feeling about this. The DPOA executive board met to discuss the matter and to vote on whether or not to revoke my membership. However, the final thought was that it might do more harm than good and could generate more sympathy for me.

PATROLMAN ACCUSES PARSELL

Jan 12, 1972

Police Slowdown Is Charged

BY MICHAEL GRAHAM
Free Press Staff Writer

A black patrolman charged Tuesday that Carl Parsell, president of the Detroit Police Officers Association, had advocated a police work slow-down.

The patrolman, James E. Crawford, 29, said that the slowdown was suggested at last Wednesday's controversial closed-door membership meeting of the DPOA, which was attended by about 1,000 Detroit policemen.

Crawford, who has won two citations and two commendations in 14 months on the force, said that DPOA attorney Norman Lippitt told him privately that a six-point "professionalism" plan on the part of Parsell was designed to make Commissioner John F. Nichols "cry uncle."

Parsell said that he had ordered more stringent adherence to police rules and admitted that this might result in fewer tickets being written. But he said this was done in the spirit of "professionalism."

"We're simply trying to do everything professionally," he insisted. "Police officers are being charged with making improper reports ... Patrolmen are being charged with overlooking parts of their job, and the blame always comes back to them."

Crawford, however, said: "He told us we should be professional to the point where it's sickening. The idea is that the general public will get sick of the lack of service."

Crawford was one of between 30 and 40 black officers who attended the DPOA meeting which was closed to reporters. He said there were racial overtones in some of Parsell's remarks.

And Crawford claimed that other black officers at the meeting agreed with him but were afraid to publicly criticize Parsell or the DPOA

"If this slowdown works, it's going to affect black people the most, because black people have the greatest need for the police," Crawford

Please turn to Page 8A, Col. 3

PATROLMAN James E. Crawford: "This is not right."

Police Accused of Slowdown Plans

Leaving work one afternoon, I had reach 35 miles per hour when I approached Fourteenth Street. Just before I got to the corner, the traffic signal changed from green to yellow. I pressed my brakes. There weren't any. I pumped and pumped. No brakes.

I knew when I parked the car that morning, the brakes were fine. I was less than twenty feet from the intersection of Fourteenth and West Grand Boulevard when the light turned red. I was still pumping like crazy and I even tried pulling the emergency brake. Nothing worked. Fourteenth is a one-way street, has three lanes of traffic, and is extremely busy during rush hour. It was rush hour.

As I got closer to the intersection, I knew I was not going to be able to stop in time, even if I had brakes. Still, I was looking for alternatives. There were none. Within a few seconds I would be in the middle of the intersection and was certain that at least one car was going to T-bone me. It was the most helpless feeling I had ever had. I decided to

75

accelerate through the intersection, hoping it would keep me from being struck. My body was rigid, my hands sweaty.

Looking to my left I could see all three lanes of traffic moving toward me. Fortunately they hadn't had time to build up enough speed to hit me. I could hear the sound of squealing tires and honking horns, but somehow I made it through unscathed. West Grand Boulevard has a five-foot wide grassy median running down the middle. I continuously pulled on and off the median until my car slowed down enough for me to ease over to the curb. I finally coasted to a stop. I raised my hood so I could check my brake fluid. There was no need. I could clearly see that the brake line leading to the brake fluid had been cut in half. As I stood there, the reality of what just happened hit me square in the face; one of my fellow officers had just tried to kill me. I walked back up to the recruiting office. Vivian gave me a ride home. I asked to be transferred back to Number 10. My wish was granted.

Rookie Patrolman James Edward Crawford

Once a Cop – Always a Cop
Nassau, Bahamas

A Shattered Dream //James E. Crawford

Chapter Five
Lie or Not to Lie
That is the Question

I returned to my regular assignment at Number 10 and was paired up with two new partners, Maurice and Ron. They were very aggressive, hard workers. Like me, they loved locking up everyone they could and they were both black. We also wrote a lot of tickets and developed a reputation of beating other officers to their radio runs and stealing their arrests. Some of the officers did not mind because they hated to do the paperwork. The others labeled us as hotdogs.

One July afternoon Maurice and I received a radio run to the third floor of an apartment building on Glynn Court. The neighbors reported hearing gunshots. We hiked our way up the steps where I stood on one side of the door armed with a shotgun and Maurice was on the other side with a carbine. We were in full uniform and our portable radios were broadcasting loud and clear. I knocked loudly on the door.

"Police officers. Open up!"

We could hear people talking inside.

"That ain't no police."

Without warning, a shotgun blast came through the fragile wooden door splattering splinters across my face. Maurice returned the fire. I immediately broke in on a radio transmission to let the dispatcher that we were under fire.

Within minutes over a dozen police cars were on the scene from our precinct and others, and they kept coming until a sergeant called them off. At least fifteen officers entered the apartment, including two sergeants. The five occupants were unceremoniously dumped from the couch to the floor. Fists were flying, bodies were being kicked, and the butts of long

79

guns were being banged against the side and back of the occupants' heads. The five were all handcuffed and taken from the apartment. One of the prisoners, handcuffed behind his back, was bumped from behind and bounced down a long flight of marble steps. The shift lieutenant arrived just as the prisoners were being taken outside.

They were a bloody mess. The lieutenant was pissed. It seemed as though he was more concerned about how he was going to explain to the chief how these prisoners got this way, than the fact that two of his officers had just been shot at. However, we weren't the ones who were bleeding. He ordered the prisoners be taken to Detroit General Hospital and their injuries photographed. He also ordered written statements from every officer at the scene, including the sergeants. All of the police officers met up in the report room at Number 10.

"Okay, you all know what to say," said John, the senior officer at the scene.

I looked at him like, "What the hell are you talking about?" He looked back at me.

"Maurice, talk to the rookie, okay?"

Maurice pulled me aside.

"What the hell is he talking about?

"I'll tell you.

Maurice then told me what to put in my report.

"You have got to be kidding."

"No, I'm not gonna write that."

"Yes, you are."

The other officers, including John, watched as Maurice and I went back and forth. I angrily left and went to the back of the station where our conversation continued. When the air cleared, all of the reports, including mine were almost verbatim. We could just have easily done one report and Xeroxed it for everyone to sign individually. Forty-five years later officers are doing the exact same thing; "He looked like

80

he was reaching for a weapon. I feared for my life, so I shot." Or "I thought I saw a shiny object in his hand." In this particular case our story was "there was a lot of confusion and commotion, it was dark inside the apartment, there were officers from several different precincts that I did not recognize and I couldn't tell who struck which prisoner."

The next day we were called in one-by-one to answer questions about the injured prisoners. Just before the first officer went in, I was pulled aside by the two sergeants.

"We are all in this together. If one falls, we all fall."

It knocked me for a loop. They were asking me to lie because technically they were in charge of the scene and they let it get out of hand. They needed to cover their asses as well as us. My written report had been very generic, but now I was going to be asked specific details. I wasn't sure what I should do. Do I lie and go against everything I have stood for all my life. Or do I tell the truth and possibly lose my job and jeopardize the jobs of several others?

If I broke from the pact and crossed that blue line, I'd have hell to pay from that day forward. If I lied, they would own me forever. It was not an easy decision to make. However, it was just that cut and dry. Either you are with us or you are against us. I was damned if I did, and damned if I didn't, and I was scared. It was time for me to go in and face the music. I slowly walked into the lieutenant's office where the two sergeants and my union rep were sitting behind a long table. I was read my Garrity Rights. Garrity says that if I lie, my lies could be used against me in a disciplinary hearing, but could not be used against me in any criminal proceeding. If they read you Miranda, your ass is in trouble. I didn't get Miranda. The first few questions were easy; they dealt with me getting the police run and the events leading up to the entry into the apartment. Then came the tough questions.

"Officer Crawford, did you observe any injuries to the prisoners?"

"Yes, sir, I did."

"Do you know how the prisoners received those injuries?"

"Yes, sir, I do."

"How were they injured?"

"They were struck by police officers."

"Which officers struck the prisoners?"

I took a deep breath and bowed my head slightly. I did not give an immediate answer.

"Officer Crawford, did you hear the question?"

"Yes, sir, I heard the question."

"And, what is your answer?"

"I cannot say with certainty which officers struck which prisoner. As I said in my report, it was dark, there was a lot of confusion, and there were officers from other precincts that I had never seen before striking the prisoners."

"Did you strike any of the prisoners?"

"No, sir, I didn't".

"I'm sorry, officer." said the lieutenant in a very loud and intimidating voice, "I didn't hear your answer."

"No, Sir. I did not strike any of the prisoners."

That part was true. I yanked one of them off the couch unceremoniously, threw him to the floor, handcuffed him behind his back, and then dragged him out of the door by the handcuffs. I did not strike any prisoner; the others did it for me. The lieutenant was pissed and gave me that "You're a lying son-of-bitch" look. He knew that if there was going to be a weak link in the chain, it would be me. All of the others had too much experience in matters like this and knew how to cover their tracks. After all, this was the infamous Tenth Precinct. The lieutenant just rolled his eyes at me.

"You're excused."

I left the room and walked straight out of the building, not saying a word to anyone. The other officers waiting to testify didn't know if I had broken down and confessed or not. One of them ran out of the building behind me. He caught up with me as I was about to enter my patrol car.

"What did you tell them?"

"I didn't snitch if that's what you're worried about."

I got in and drove off. Everyone stuck to their guns and told the same story as we had agreed to. Eventually, the matter was dropped for lack of evidence. The prisoners were also released because it could not be determined which one of the five had fired the shotgun through the door. I guess you could call this one a tie.

What we had just done is typical. Officers across this nation have a "Handbook" in cases like this. Of course it is a virtual handbook where nothing is actually written down, but by word of mouth it spells out what you are supposed to say and do in each situation. Instructions for this particular incident can be found in Chapter One, "How to Cover up Your Fellow Officer's Criminality with a Lie."

I was hard to get along with the next few days. I had just compromise everything I stood for all these years to protect a bunch of cops who beat the shit out of five suspects, pushing one down the steps handcuffed behind his back. Their argument to me was how could I feel sorry for a person who just shot at me through a door? You have to pause here a minute and truly digest what just happened, and then ask yourself what you would have done in this situation? This is not a made up story, this is how it is out there for both rookies and veteran officers from day one to the last day on the job. Things eventually got back to normal. Maurice, Ron, and I went back to our old routine of catching crooks. This is why I joined the department in the first place, and this was what makes my day, taking the bad guys off the street. I was back to fulfilling my childhood dream and loving every minute of it.

In our travels, Maurice introduced me to a close friend of his named Edgar. Edgar was a locksmith by trade and also installed burglar alarms in homes and businesses. After moving from my apartment to my new home, I had him install mine.

Edgar was leaning toward joining the department, and Maurice did all he could to get him to do it. It reminded me of my old teaching days at Northern High when Felix recruited me into the police department. Like me, all Edgar needed was a little push. Edgar finally gave in and became of one Detroit's finest. Edgar was not on the job long before he was assigned to plainclothes duty, a rarity in those days. He was assigned to a special detail under one of the best known bureau commanders. They mostly investigated white collar crimes.

Shortly after I joined the DPD, Detroit residents were beginning to take sides due to all of the killings of young, unarmed, black men by the S.T.R.E.S.S. unit (Stop the Robberies Enjoy Safe Streets) which was created after the 1967 riots. Detroit's crime rate had experienced a huge spike, especially in street robberies. The citizens demanded action. Officers posing as drunks, homeless people, and the elderly were positioning themselves to be robbed by street thugs. As soon as the suspect made his attempted crime the officer would identify himself and make the arrest. Backup officers were always nearby. S.T.R.E.S.S was working for a while.

Officers were reducing crime and they were getting tons of guns off the street. But then there came a rash of fatal shootings. They began to pile up. The mugging "victims" or decoys, were reporting that they were being attacked and were in fear for their life and had no choice but to resort to the use of fatal force. The shooting deaths of suspects were coming fast and furious, and in my personal conversations with both S.T.R.E.S.S. and regular patrol officers, the carnage did not seem to bother the officers. They saw it as getting the bad guys off the street. During the next several years over twenty Detroit citizens would be killed by the

S.T.R.E.S.S. unit. All but two of them were black. My fellow officers and I clearly understood that S.T.R.E.S.S. was nothing more than an execution squad.

One S.T.R.E.S.S officer was involved in twelve of those shootings, five of them fatal. Eventually he was charged with murder. The impetus for his murder charge was the knife he planted on his last victim. Even though the police lab found hairs from the officer's cat inside the knife, the officer was still found not-guilty by a jury. A psychiatrist testifying for the defense painted a picture of an officer in constant fear for his life, so he planted the knife to keep from being convicted of a crime he felt he had not committed.

I interviewed several of my former classmates from the police academy who became members of the S.T.R.E.S.S. unit. They told me that the internal strife between black and white officers within the S.T.R.E.S.S. unit so intense that the seven squads on each of the two shifts eventually had to be divided by race and each squad became either all white or all black. One of my sources told me that the white officers had no problem mistreating or manhandling black suspects in front of black officers, nor did they have a problem with the frequent use of the word nigger. One of my sources sent me the following e-mail:

"The basic premise for STRESS was noble, to stop the robberies, which at the time were numerous and often occurred in the areas we worked. When the unit first started, we witnessed all types of crimes committed in our immediate view and made many good arrests. The crooks hadn't got the word on us. But as time went on the racism emerged more than the desire to arrest criminals and the pickings got slimmer due to the many arrests that these plainclothes people were making.

As the arrests slowed, the older white officers didn't want to work with the younger black officers. The reason was that we didn't go along with their trumped up charges against people who had not committed a crime or they did not catch in the act of committing a crime. Sometimes they would try to make arrests on persons in the vicinity of a reported crime just to try and keep their "stats" up. Some of the "crew chiefs" were so stupid or ignorant of the law, they would make blatant false arrests. I remember one crew beating some white suspects and telling them "you don't have any rights," because you are Canadian."

Detroit, Michigan, and Windsor, Ontario both border the Detroit River. Literally thousands of Americans and Canadians cross back and forth each day either on the Ambassador Bridge or through the Windsor Tunnel.

It was not just the white squads at S.T.R.E.S.S. who were trigger happy, one of the black squads was not much better. They treated black suspects just as bad as the white squads. One of the black squad's encounters ended in a shootout with members of the county sheriff's office who were also working undercover. All eight officers involved from both agencies were black and in plainclothes. By the time I arrived on the scene, it was pure chaos. Members from both agencies were pointing fingers at each other for what happened, and had to be separated. One of the deputies was killed during the exchange of gunfire between the two police agencies. This shooting strained the relationship between officers from the Detroit Police Department and the Wayne County Sheriff's Department for years.

This blatant disregard for black lives wasn't or isn't just a S.T.R.E.S.S. unit issue. We are seeing it all across the country on a daily basis, including in my own county where deputies fired 121 rounds into the car of an unarmed black man. Their actions were deemed justified by the county sheriff, who is also black. My interview with a former high ranking veteran officer from the Orange County Sheriff's Department was equally chilling. He recalled incidents earlier in his career where deputies who were involved in fatal shootings of a black suspects would actually brag about how they "lit his ass up" or "I smoked that son-of-a-bitch"

Forty-five years later, the mentality of Detroit's S.T.R.E.S.S. officers is shared by police officers all around the country and the shooting of unarmed black men has reached epidemic proportions with the majority of the officers are getting away scot-free. Some Detroit officers had the audacity to brag about getting their "five days", the amount of time they would be given off back then while the shooting was being investigated.

Months after I arrived at Number 10, Officer Gilbert was involved in a fatal shooting. He was an old veteran and seemed to be very upset and remorseful about what he had done, unlike many of the younger officers. I made the mistake of repeating a statement to him that I had heard several times in my short time there.

"Well, at least you got your five days."

Officer Gilbert gave me a look that I had never seen before and don't ever want to see again. There was anger in his voice.

"I just killed a man!"

He rolled his eyes at me and turned away. I felt about three feet tall. He was the exception rather than the rule. I never said that again to anyone nor did I participate in the end of the year "death pool". The national and local media had labeled Detroit as the Murder Capital. During the last week in December each year, the officers actually set up a pool predicting the number of murders Detroit would end up with by year's end. The officer who came closest without going over won the money. You would actually hear officers say with a smile, "Three more and I win the pot!" It was a sickness that permeated several units in the department. Black lives did not matter!

Once a Cop – Always a Cop
Buckingham Palace

Chapter Six
The Task Force

Near the end of the summer Maurice began to have problems staying awake. His enthusiasm had also diminished markedly. When I asked him about it he said that he was working a second job. Things began to get worse and staying awake on patrol had now become a chore. I was concerned.

"Partner, you're going to have to give up that second job before you get one of us killed. This is the second time this week you missed a knife on somebody you were searching."

"I know. I want to talk to you about that second job."

He then posed a very unusual question.

"If you knew that officers at this precinct were dealing drugs and protecting drug dealers, would you do anything about it?"

I gave him the Grand Rapids look.

"Yes, I probably would."

"If it was somebody you were friends with and worked with every day, would you still turn them in?"

"Where are we going with this, Maurice? Please don't tell me you are involved in drugs. I've already had three partners arrested; I don't need a fourth one."

He laughed.

"No, I'm not involved in drugs, okay? I just needed to know what you would do. We'll talk about it tomorrow. I have to check with someone first."

I didn't get a lot of sleep that night wondering what the hell was going on. The next day after our shift ended he took me to a house in the Twelfth Precinct. As soon as the man opened the door I recognized him. He was a lieutenant named George.

"Lieutenant, this is my partner, James Crawford, the one I have been telling you about." George extended his hand.

"Hello, sir."

"Hello, Crawford, I've heard a lot about you."

"I hope it was all good,"

"It was. "I hear you can be trusted."

"Yes, sir, I can." I quickly added, "as long as I don't have to do anything illegal."

"Trust me. What you will be doing will not be illegal. Has Maurice told you what's going on and why I asked him to bring you here?"

"No sir, he hasn't. I have no idea why I am here."

"Did he mention anything about officers at your precinct being involved in drug trafficking?"

"Yes, he did, but very little else."

"Drug trafficking by police officers at Tenth Precinct is pervasive and a special task force had been appointed directly by the police commissioner to investigate. The task force is working in conjunction the State Attorney's office. Maurice and I, along with several others are part of this task force investigating the corruption and we would like you to join us. I understand you have some very strong principles and your level of honesty is quite high. On this detail, you may have to compromise some of those principles and turn your back on some dishonest things you may see other cops do. Do you think you can handle that?"

"I don't know. Are you saying that if I see crimes being committed by my fellow officers, I'm supposed to turn my back and pretend I didn't see it?

"Yes. But, you will make an official report on what you see and it will be dealt with at a later time. There may also be a time or two when you'll witness a street crime like a street robbery or car burglary and cannot take action because you are on surveillance."

"I'm not sure if I can do that."

"Well, you let Maurice know and we'll talk about it again."

Maurice and I left and sat out front talking about it. He assured me that violating my principles now would reap great benefits in the future. He encouraged me to join the task force.

"Oh, by the way, the reason I've been so sleepy lately is that when I get off work at the precinct, I work with the task force until three or four in the morning. If you join, you'll probably have to do the same."

I knew that wouldn't go over very well with Lola. She and I definitely had to talk this over before I gave the lieutenant my decision. Things had gotten a little better at home. I didn't know what kind of disruption this would cause if I joined.

"I've been asked to join a special task force investigating crooked cops at Number 10. It means I may have to work some extra hours. What do you think?"

"Investigating other cops? You'll be working at Internal Affairs, the unit that every cop hates?

"No, this is a separate investigation. We were all handpicked and we will be working directly for the commissioner and alongside the Attorney General's office."

"You'll still be investigating cops that you work with everyday?"

"Yes."

"From what I've seen on TV, I don't think it is a good move. Think about what you are getting yourself into."

91

I hesitated before giving Maurice an answer. After a week or so I said yes. Because of Maurice's reputation as a street-wise, pot-smoking cop who grew up in Detroit, and my reputation as being naive and 'super honest', the lieutenant had us playing good/cop bad cop.

If we witnessed anything illegal being done by the officers and had a problem with it, it was Maurice's job to side with the officer and hold me in check. It didn't take long for me to see my first act of police thievery. It happened one night when Maurice and I backed up another crew on an arrest. One of the officers making the arrest, Tony, had a reputation of being one of the biggest thieves in the department. Why he had never been caught was quite a mystery to me. A prisoner Tony had arrested was being processed at the precinct lock up. They asked the prisoner to remove everything from his pockets and lay it on the counter.

One of the items he removed was an expensive looking gold watch. Tony's eyes lit up like a Christmas tree. He commented several time on how nice it would look on his wrist. After patting the man down and filling out the fingerprint card, Tony turned the prisoner over to the turnkey. Just before the prisoner was taken to his cell, he was asked to sign his property ticket which itemized everything taken from him. He signed the ticket and began walking back toward his cell. After taking a few steps, the prisoner suddenly stopped.

"Wait a minute. Wait a minute. My watch was not listed on the ticket."

"What watch?" asked the turnkey.

"The gold watch I was wearing when I came in."

"I didn't see a gold watch."

"You weren't there when I took it off."

"I don't know anything about a gold watch, but I do know I've got to put you in a cell".

"Wait a minute. Can't I talk to the captain or somebody? That watch cost over three hundred dollars."

The turnkey brought the prisoner back to front desk.

"What's the problem?"

"Sarge, this guy said he had a three hundred dollar gold watch when he came in. Now he says it's missing."

The sergeant looked at the property ticket.

"It's not listed. Did you see the watch?"

"No sir, I didn't."

"He signed his property ticket, didn't he?"

"Yes, Sir, he signed it right here, pointing to the signature.

"Well, as far as I'm concerned, he didn't have a watch. Take him back to his cell."

"Wait a minute sergeant. I had the watch when I came in. You can ask the officers that arrested me. They saw it."

"Didn't you sign the property ticket?"

"Yes, but I didn't read it first. I just thought it would be on there. I never thought the police would steal my watch. Can't you call the officers in and ask them?"

"I'm not going to call them off the street, but I will ask them next time they come into the station."

"Please do that. Please.

The turnkey took the prisoner back to his cell and for the moment the incident was forgotten. I was standing at the front desk during the entire conversation between the sergeant and the prisoner. I had a good idea where the watch went. A few minutes later Tony came back into the station and went into the report room. Ignoring the instructions given to me by the task force lieutenant, I mentioned the missing watch to Tony.

"I don't know why you're telling me about his fucking watch. I didn't take it."

"You saw the watch, Tony. I was there when he took it off, and so were you."

"Are you accusing me of stealing the man's watch?"

"I'm not accusing you of anything, but if asked, I will say that I saw the watch and so did you."

Tony and I exchanged glares for a few seconds, and then I left. When I told Maurice about the watch incident he blew up.

"Why did you say something to Tony about the watch? Didn't the lieutenant tell us not to say or do anything?"

"Yes, but I just couldn't let him steal the man's watch and not say anything. You know he will never get that watch back."

"Yes you can. And, if you're gonna work this detail you have no choice. So you better get used to it."

I hated it already, but I knew Maurice was right. Just before the end of the shift, I walked behind the desk and checked the prisoner's property again. The watch was there. I had just been given my first task force integrity test and I failed it miserably. I knew right then that watching officers commit crimes and not saying anything was not going to be easy, and I realized that I had gotten myself into another mess.

Tony was not the only officer at Number 10 stealing from prisoners' property. We also had a doorman, aka turnkey, who had been on the job over twenty years. He was arrested by Internal Affairs for stealing money and other items from prisoner's property. After receiving a tip, not from me, they set him up big time and he took the bait.

Thefts by officers were not limited to just the prisoners. On payday night, the clerk at each precinct would pick up our payroll checks from downtown. He would sort them at the precinct, make a sign in sheet, and place the checks in a box at the front desk. Officers drifted in after 7:00 p.m. to pick them up. An officer picking up his or her check would thumb through the checks until he found his or hers. A bar across the street from Number 10 offered check cashing night.

Most precincts had the same set up. For a small fee the bartender cashed the checks and the cops guzzled down the booze. On more than one occasion checks disappeared between downtown and the time the officer came to pick it up at Number 10. Cops were stealing checks from other cops. This prompted a policy change where only the supervisor on desk duty had access to the checks.

Detroit police officers have a network like no other organization in the world. If something involving an officer happens in the First Precinct, by day's end every precinct, bureau and section in the department will know about it, and the details will vary like you can't believe. During the next few months rumors of a grand jury probe into possible police corruption at the Number 10 began to surface and grew like wildfire.

The rumors said officers from Internal Affairs were planted at the precinct. These same types of rumors had surfaced in the past, and each time they were true. Officers had no reason not to believe this rumor wasn't true this time. As the rumors persisted, the names of officers possibly involved in the investigation began to surface. Tension heightened at the precinct and officers began to polarize. The two names that came up the most as spies were Maurice and me. We both knew that it would be just a matter of time before the shit hit the fan. One of the officers gave a house party and surprisingly Maurice and I were invited. As soon as we walked in the door we found ourselves surrounded by several officers.

"You two aren't wearing a wire, are you?"

"A wire?"

They actually patted us down, in a joking manner. Maurice and I knew right then that it was over. We stayed a few minutes long and then left. We told the lieutenant what happened and he had us transferred the next day. On paper Maurice and I were transferred to the vice section because officially the task force did not exist.

The code name for this non-existent task force was Detail 318. From that day forward we reported to eleventh floor office of the State Attorney General's office downtown.

Although it was a joint operation, tension between the two agencies, the DPD and the State Attorney General's office, was high and trust was nonexistent. It was kind of like the trust between the FBI and local law enforcement. Vic, a patrolman, and Melvin, a sergeant, were the other two members of the DPD team. Howard, Walter, John and two secretaries made up the State Attorney's staff.

In most cases police corruption issues are handled by Internal Affairs, but that wasn't the case here, and the folks at Internal Affairs did not appreciate it. Their egos had been bruised when the commissioner bypassed them and initiated his own handpicked team. They didn't take it sitting down. The head of Internal Affairs went to the police commissioner and expressed his displeasure over being snubbed. On more than one occasion, we found members from Internal Affairs following us. Once, I walked over to their surveillance car and I handed the I A officer my itinerary for the day. On another occasion I got behind the officer who had been following me and began following him. It turned out to be one hell of a chase until I finally backed off. Frequent leaks to the local newspapers fueled the battle between the three agencies, the task force, the State Attorney, and I.A., with each accusing the other of making the leak. The whole scenario was becoming extremely childish. Maurice and I spent the next two months on surveillance across the street from Number 10. Officers I had worked with for the last year or more were now being watched by us through binoculars, and their every movement was being recorded.

"This shit sucks."

"What the hell did you expect when you joined this detail?" "I don't know. Not this. I guess I made my decision too quickly. I should have listened to my wife."

"Well, it's kinda late for that now. You made your decision and now you're just going to have to live with it."

Once the task force was exposed, death threats came in on a daily basis; there were so many that we actually kept track of them in a binder. Most of the threats simply warned us to watch our ass, while others actually threatened us with physical harm. I took them seriously, especially with the incident with the brakes incident still very fresh in my mind. What made the threats even more personal was a conversation I had with an old girlfriend named Louise. Louise and I met when I first moved to Detroit. We dated a few times and then I lost contact with her for a few years until I ran into her at a supermarket.

"James Crawford, I don't believe it. Where the hell have you been?"

"I've been around. How have you been doing?"

"I'm doing fine. I'm gotten a little fat I last saw you, but I'm doing okay."

"You're still looking good."

"Jimmy, I need to talk to you. It's important."

I walked her to her car and as we were loading in the groceries she dropped the bomb on me.

"I'm not sure if you know it or not, but I'm dating Richard."

"No, I didn't."

"The story is that you and some special task force are investigating him and others at the Tenth Precinct for drug trafficking."

"Damn! Is there anybody in Detroit that doesn't know about this?"

"Let me tell you, he hates you, Maurice, and he hates that lieutenant's guts. Please watch yourself. He's using heavy right now and I believe he will hurt you if he gets a chance. He hangs around with some very shady characters. And hurting or killing fellow cops won't bother him one bit. He will do it if he gets a chance, okay?"

Richard and I had worked together several times. He had a reputation of being on the wrong side of the law and hanging out with known criminals; however, he was never caught or charged with anything.

"Thanks, Louise, I appreciate the warning. And, I will watch my ass, I promise."

"I know you're wondering why I'm still with him."

"It did cross my mind."

"I don't know myself. I still love him. I know that sounds crazy"

"Okay, Louise, take care and thanks again for the warning."

I left her car visibly shaken. My hands were trembling, my throat and mouth were dry, and my heart was pounding so hard I thought it was going to pop out through my chest. If there had been any doubt before about the validity of the death threats, those doubts had just been removed. I recorded my conversation with Louise in the binder and told the rest of the team. One of my former classmates from 70K, Craig, was a member of Number 10's narcotics squad. He was the suspected bag man for the squad. If I had known this when I joined the task force it definitely would have made a difference. He and I were still good friends, and on occasion we spent time together off-duty.

Our wives had also become good friends. When the lieutenant learned of our friendship, he asked me to approach Craig, feel him out, and see if he was willing to cooperate with the task force in exchange for immunity.

"I can't do that, Sir."

"What do you mean you can't do that? Whose side are you on?"

"He and I are friends. Our wives are friends. I'm at his house a lot, and he's at mine."

"What will you do if we get into a shootout and he's on the other side?"

"I'm not worried about that. The chances of that happening are very remote."

"We have enough evidence to arrest him right now. He may want to save his own ass. If you're his friend like you say, you'll be giving him a chance to stay out of prison."

"I don't know. I—I—"

"It sounds to me like you have your loyalties mixed up. Think about it. We're trying to build a case here. We need all the help we can get. Your friend Craig can help us and himself at the same time."

"I'm sorry, lieutenant, but that's not something I want to do."

Before Maurice and I left the building, the lieutenant called him over. I could hear their conversation, which may have been intentional.

"I'm worried about Crawford. I don't know if he can be trusted anymore. I think that starting tomorrow I'll keep him busy in the office on paperwork. You and Vic can work the streets." One of the allegations being investigated was that instead of paying their informants with cash, the narcotics officers were taking part of the dope they confiscated and giving it to the informant as payment. This was not only against department policy, it was also a criminal act. Technically, this made the officers dope dealers.

One of the informants being paid off in drugs had the street name of "Shooter". Shooter became a double agent. He made dope purchases for the Number 10 Narcotics Squad, and received money from us for snitching on their activities.

One night Maurice and I left the lieutenant's house and headed for Number 10. On the way we received a call from Shooter. He told us that he had information and wanted us to pick him up at the usual place. When we met him, he told us about a large drug bust that was about to go down in Number 10 and thought we may want to observe it. He said he did not know how much of the dope was going to make it to the evidence room and how much they were going to keep for themselves. We gave him his weekly cash payment and then he asked us to drop him off on Twelfth Street.

"I'll be right back."

I looked at Maurice.

"Be right back?"

"Where's he going?"

"You don't want to know."

"Yes, I do!"

Maurice did not say another word. He just smiled. Realizing where we were, a light bulb came on in my head.

"Wait a minute. He's going to the dope house, isn't he?"

Silence.

"We just paid him off, we took him to the dope house, and now we are going to drive him back home with dope in his pocket in our police car? You've got to be kiddin' me?"

"Hey, we need his testimony. Welcome to the real world."

"This is bullshit. I can't do this. And, this isn't the first time you have done this, is it?"

"Stop bitching. Those are our orders. Like it or not, we have no choice."

"You might not have a choice, but I sure as hell do."

The next day I was assigned to desk duty. It was boring as hell, but it gave me time to think about my future with the task force and the department. That childhood dream of mine was turning into a nightmare. Vic was now Maurice's new partner. I had no problem with that. I asked the lieutenant how much longer he thought the task force would be in operation.

"Until we finish the job."

I asked to be transferred. My request was denied. The tension and uneasiness at the office continued to grow. Vic had also had it and was ready to move on. He asked the lieutenant to transfer him back to a precinct, but his request was also denied. After four weeks of doing nothing but paperwork, I was finally given an assignment that took me out of the office.

"Gentlemen, we are about to do something that has never been done in the history of the Detroit Police Department. We are going to conduct a raid on the Tenth Precinct. A search warrant for the precinct's narcotics office has been authorized and secured by the Commissioner. We're leaving in five minutes."

"Lieutenant, I can't do this."

"You don't have a choice."

Everyone from both units, the State Attorney General and DPD, took part in the raid. Twenty minutes after leaving the task force office we reached Number 10. With the lieutenant leading the way, we marched in one behind the other. We looked like the 82nd Airborne. Everyone in the lobby and behind the desk stopped in their tracks. The lieutenant handed the search warrant to the sergeant on the desk and we proceeded into the precinct's narcotics office where everyone, including supervisors, was ordered out. We conducted a desk by desk, drawer by drawer, and shelf by shelf search looking for drugs and anything else we could find that was illegal.

101

I don't remember opening one single drawer. I was just there. According to Shooter unreported drugs were there, drugs that should have been placed on evidence and taken down to the main narcotics section for processing. We found the drugs along with a couple of guns and several police reports. We marched back out just like we marched in. The looks on the precinct officers faces are ones I will never forget. I had never been so embarrassed and ashamed in all my life. The raid not only made the local news channels, the story was picked up by all three major networks; ABC, CBS, and NBC.

After returning to the task force office, the lieutenant, the sergeant, Maurice, and those from the Attorney General's office were in a jubilant mood. They had scored a big victory.

"Are you all happy now? Don't you want to call a news conference and show off your goodies?"

Everyone in the room just looked at me. They knew it was best just to leave it alone, and they did.

The news of the raid quickly spread through the network, and within twenty-four hours every cop in Detroit knew what happened. I received a few calls at home warning me to be careful. These were from friends who were concerned about me. There were also some that were not so friendly.

The raid on the precinct was the last straw for me. I knew I had to get away from the task force no one was going to stop me, including the lieutenant. I had never had my loyalty or integrity challenged as much as it had been on this detail. I also had never been as alienated by my co-workers as I had been on this detail.

Another first for me was that I had to write everything down in code so that my fellow officers couldn't decipher my notes, in case they found them. This included telephone numbers, names, addresses and locations. Everything was in code, like something from a James Bond movie. What the hell had I gotten myself into?

After the raid I told Vic about us taking Shooter to the dope house and Tony stealing the watch.

"If you think that was bad, you should have been here the other night when they hung the guy out of the window."

"Out of the window? What are you talking about?"

"Crawford, they hung the motherfucker out of the window by his ankles until he told them what they wanted. I kid you not."

Vic raised his right.

"I swear to God."

"From the eleventh floor?"

"Yes, from the eleventh floor."

"I don't know about you Vic, but I'm outta here."

I internalized much of what was going on and didn't take it home to Lola. As a result, I ended up with an ulcer. I did not want Lola to worry about my safety any more than she did already, and although she was not a vindictive person, I also did not want her silent version of "I told you so" to emerge. She pointed out the difficulties I might face when we first talked about me joining the task force and I joined anyway. This one was on me. Vic and I typed up official transfer requests and a letter requesting an immediate meeting with the commissioner.

I hand delivered it during my lunch hour. The commissioner agreed to see us. Vic and I explained the situation. The commissioner told us that he didn't want anyone on the task force that did not want to be there; it was too important an assignment, and he didn't want it compromised. The operation had already cost tens of thousands of dollars and so far produced little results. He said he had to hear the other side of the story and then make a decision. A week later, Vic was transferred to the Court Section. Two weeks later I was transferred to the 13th Precinct.

On the Streets of Jerusalem
Once a Cop – Always a Cop

Cairo Airport

Chapter Seven
The Family Misfit

T he word of my impending transfer quickly reached the Thirteenth Precinct. They were waiting for me. I had no idea what type of reception I was going to receive and did not know what to expect. I was hoping it would be good, but was not overly optimistic. It had only been a short time since the raid on Number 10 and officers throughout the department knew the threats against me were still coming. Some of the officers I was about to join may have been the ones to send them.

I waited until the very last minute before entering the building. As I walked in, all eyes seemed to be focused on me. It was as if I was wearing a space helmet and dressed as Robocop. I smiled and nodded at a few of the officers I recognized. Some of them responded with a weak and halfhearted wave of their hand. I walked to the front desk and asked the sergeant on duty where I was supposed to report. He told me that the precinct inspector wanted to talk to me first and to just have a seat. An inspector is equivalent to a captain. Sitting on the bench across from the front desk, I felt more like someone waiting to bond out a prisoner than a police officer waiting for his next assignment.

As more officers reported to duty, I felt like each and every one of them went out of their way to walk by the bench or to peer at me from across the room. Maybe I was just a little paranoid. After about twenty minutes, the sergeant told me that the Inspector was ready to see me.

I removed my hat and placed it under my left arm before walking into the inspector's office. Subordinates are not allowed to wear their hat when entering the offices of command officers. Removal of the hat and placing it under the arm is the military way of saluting in his or her office. As I entered the room I saw a middle aged, well-built man with salt and pepper hair sitting behind the desk. He rose from his seat, introduced himself and extended his hand. His name was Frank and his vocabulary was not for the meek, mild, or faint of heart.

"Welcome aboard. What made you decide to come to my precinct?"

"I talked to Vic and he said you were a good and fair man to work for."

"You know everybody here thinks you're from Internal Affairs."

"Yes, sir. I got a whiff of that already."

"Then you also know they don't like you and are afraid of you."

"Yes, sir, I kinda expected that."

"It's not going to be easy here. Cops are some funny ass people. They think it's okay to bust motherfuckers on the street selling dope, but if you bust one of them for doing the same shit, they consider you a traitor."

"I know, I'm finding that out the hard way."

"As long as you do your job I don't give a fuck where you're from. Some of these sons-of--bitches need to be in jail.

I admire your courage for taking on such an assignment so early in your career. I hope everything works out for you. Report to the lieutenant and he'll give you your new assignment.

Yes, sir. Thank you, sir."

The lieutenant hadn't come in yet so the sergeant gave me a grand tour of the precinct and assigned me a locker. As we passed through the different sections of the building the sergeant introduced me to fellow officers and to other sergeants. The reception was lukewarm, but no one was rude, nor did anyone make any unsavory comments. By the time we got back to the special operations office, my new partner had arrived. His name was Donald. He was a tall, thin, young redbone who looked like he had just stepped off a college campus.

"Donald, this is James Crawford, your new partner."

"It's nice to meet you. I've heard a lot about you,"

He had a big smile on his face.

"Yes, I'm sure you have. Did they also tell you what a nice guy I am, and how meek and mild I am?"

We both laughed.

"Don't worry about these people around here. A month from now you'll just be one of the fellows."

We had an even bigger laugh. Donald went over our duties and gave me a map of the precinct, pointing out the high crime areas.

"This is where we will concentrate our patrols."

I was delighted. I was finally going to get back into doing what I loved the most, fighting crime on the street. Things went fairly well for Donald and me for the next month or so. We made tons of arrests and seemed to work very well together. We were even called in one afternoon by the lieutenant for some kudos.

"I want to congratulate you two on the good job you're doing out there.

You have made some very good arrests. Keep up the good work."

"Damn!"

I couldn't believe what I had just heard. I was grinning from ear to ear. That good news lasted about one week. Donald informed me that before I had arrived he had asked for the job as the precinct's crime prevention officer, which was about to become vacant. He had been told that morning

107

that the officer who held the job had finally turned in his papers, and the job was now his. Donald had to shadow the outgoing officer the final week before his retirement. I was now without a partner. I had grown to like him and we had developed a great working relationship in a very short period of time. I hated to see it come to an end.

The next day the lieutenant notified me that not only was I losing my partner, but that I was being assigned to the power shift that operated from 7:00 pm to 3:00 am.

I didn't like the switch and I knew it was going to cause more problems at home. Things had been getting worse rather than better over the past few months. Before I could fully digest the loss of my partner and my transfer to the power shift, I received a message to return to the station as soon as possible. The minute I walked in, I was handed a message by the desk clerk. It was from Lola and marked "Urgent". My heart began to pound. I hadn't been this nervous since my talk with Louise. I called home immediately. The phone rang at least five times. Lola always answered on the first or second ring. I knew it was serious. A sobbing and nearly inaudible Lola finally answered.

"Lola? What's wrong?"

My daddy died."

"What?"

"My daddy died."

"What happened?"

"He was conducting a funeral and fell over and died of a heart attack at the cemetery."

"I'm so sorry. I'll be home in a few minutes."

I notified the lieutenant of my father-in-law's death and asked for a few days off to attend the funeral in New York. He told me to take all the time I needed. I rushed home as my mind went from one extreme to another. This was the first time either one of us had experienced death in the immediate family since my grandmother died nearly fourteen years ago.

Both of my parents were still living as well as my eleven brothers and sisters.

With our marriage rapidly declining, I had been thinking about moving out of the house. I didn't know what affect her father's death would have on that decision. I was hoping it would help bring us back together. Lola and I spent the next week in New York taking care of family matters. Lola's father was a very popular funeral director and had one of the largest funerals ever seen in Harlem. Limousines were lined up for blocks.

My mother-in-law and I had never gotten along, and her husband's death did not bring us any closer together. After coming back from the funeral, things between Lola and I seemed to be getting a little better but then took a turn south. My thoughts about leaving resurfaced, but now was not the time.

The day after returning from New York I reported back to the Thirteenth Precinct and my new shift. Within minutes I could feel a difference in attitudes than when Donald and I worked together. No smiles, no handshakes, and the long and boisterous conversations in the squad room suddenly stopped when I walked into the room. That was not a comfortable feeling. The sergeant introduced me to my new squad members individually; only one or two bothered to look up, and no one extended a hand, including the supervisors. There was an eerie atmosphere over the room. It was obvious everyone was uptight and uncomfortable with me being there. Questions I asked were answered with one word, the pointing of a finger, or the nodding of the head.

My new partner was Jack, a short heavy-set man six years younger than me but with two more years on the job. Jack wasted no time in letting me know how he felt about being my partner.

"Look, I'm going to tell you up front, I did not ask to be your partner. I just happen to be low in seniority and got stuck with you. Folks around here are scared of you, including me. The word is that there is a contract out on you and believe me it is for real. Nobody wants to be with you when you get hit. I know I don't. I have a wife and kids."

I was caught completely off guard by Jack's comment and really didn't know what to say. Throughout the night Jack constantly questioned me about the task force and insisted that I was still actually assigned to Internal Affairs.

"I really don't care about the fact that you're from I. A. I haven't done anything wrong. I'm just worried about getting my ass blown away working with you."

During the next few weeks we spent a lot of time in the station. Reports that normally took twenty minutes to fill out were now taking an hour or more. Every time we went back on the street, Jack would constantly be looking around to see if anyone was watching us or following us. He would even check the backseat each time before we got into the car. I had had enough.

"Jack, I've listened to your bitching for the last three weeks and I'm sick of it. If someone is going to hit me, they know where I live, what time I go to work, what time I get off, what time I go to the market and every other Goddamn thing there is to know about me. Why in the hell would they shoot me while I was on duty with cops all around me? You know, you're just a fat-ass, chicken shit, Uncle Tom asshole who wants to be one of the boys. And; from what I've seen so far, you're no prize to work with your damn self. You sure as hell can't catch anybody with your fat ass. Who the hell are you to be picky?" Jack was as dumfounded with my comments as I had been when we first met. He did not open his mouth for the next several minutes.

Humor is a wonderful remedy, and a humorous moment helped to ease our situation. A woman we pulled over for running a red light did not have a driver's license. She looked to be eight plus months pregnant. I went to the driver's side.

110

"I need your license, registration, and proof of insurance."

"I don't have it. My husband took it so I wouldn't drive."

"Then why are you driving?

"I wanted some cookies and he said I had to wait until half time of the game he is watching."

"I can't let you drive away from here knowing you don't have a license. If you hit and kill someone, they are going to sue you, me, and everybody else. Is there someone other than you husband you can call to come get you?"

"I'll call my sister."

There was a telephone booth on the corner. Cell phones had not made their large scale debut as of yet.

"I'm going to be watching you from up the street and pregnant or not, if you do drive off I'm going to lock you up. Do you understand that?"

"Yes, sir, officer. I won't drive, I promise."

Jack and I got about a half block away when I looked in the rear view mirror.

"Jack, take a look in the mirror."

The woman had made a U-Turn and was hauling ass down the street. We both cracked up.

The detail for the next day is posted before the end of shift. Whenever Jack had the day off officers closely checked the roster to see if they were scheduled to work with me. If so, often they would call in sick. After working eight hours with Jack and the rest of that gang, playing the happy and amorous husband at home was difficult. Had I been able to share my work problems, fears, and concerns with Lola, it may have brought us closer together. But, how could I tell her that nearly everyone at work hated my guts and did not want to work with me, especially when she did not want me on the force in the first place. In the beginning I kept my misery to myself. Later, I began to bring some of it home, which took its toll on our marriage. We were becoming more impatient with each other, often causing me to snap at her when it was

111

totally unnecessary. I guess I was just ready to get out. Other than bowling and running, I did not have a lot of outside activities.

When I was teaching Lola and I visited friends on occasion, went to parties, took Tracey to the park and on short trips. Since joining the force we did very little socializing. Not only was going to work no longer fun, coming home wasn't either. My dream job wasn't all I thought it would be.

That conversation I had with Louise was still fresh in my mind and because of the treatment I was getting from my colleagues, as a precaution, I began to keep a diary. I did not hide the diary and wrote in it openly. It was my way of telling everyone to back off. This was another one of the times when I knew I was the one making the problem worse, but I didn't care. I also carried a tape recorder whenever I worked a one-man car. Before I got out of my patrol car, I said the license plate number, make, model, and color of the car into the recorder. I kept it going while I was out of the car. This was no way to live.

Not everyone showed their ass. Howard, a twenty-three year veteran who did not take any BS from anyone, and who had faced the same type of ostracism years ago, befriended me.

"Crawford, these guys are treacherous. They are doing shit out here on the street that can send their ass to prison. It has been this way for years.

With you being from Internal, they are scared, and they will set your ass up in a heartbeat. Just be careful; watch your back and cover your ass every chance you get."

"Howard, I am not from Internal."

"It doesn't matter, they think you are and that's all that counts. Just hang in there, everything will be okay. I got your back."

I had no reason to doubt him and often went to him for advice. He did have my back, and I was extremely grateful. While working the task force I had two of my vacations cancelled. I decided that now would be a good time to take one of them. I didn't get any resistance from my bosses. My vacation started two days before Memorial Day. I decided to go home to visit my parents.

I hadn't seen them in a while and I needed a break from all the tension and time to think about my rapidly deteriorating marriage. Parents seem to know when things are wrong with their children, especially mothers. I can certainly feel it when something is going wrong in my daughters' lives. I wasn't in the house five minutes when my mother picked up on the fact that I was troubled.

"You don't look very good, is everything okay?"

"Yeah, Ma, I'm just tired from the drive up here."

"Are you and Lola having problems? I noticed that you didn't bring her with you."

"Yes, everything is okay. Really. Would I lie to you?"

"Yes, you would if you thought I would worry about you."

"Everything's okay. I swear."

"You know a mother can always tell when something is wrong. You can always come back home if things get too rough. It's nothing to be ashamed of."

"Ma, I am thirty-one years old! No man goes back home to live with his parents at that age."

After a hearty meal, visits with some of my old friends, and a good night's sleep, I packed up and headed back to Detroit. As I passed the state capitol in Lansing I noticed that my left front wheel was beginning to shimmy. I had noticed something on the way down, but just shook it off. I rolled down the window and listened to see if I could hear any noises. I didn't hear a thing. However, the further I drove, the more the car shook. Travelling at sixty miles per hour, it was not a good feeling.

113

I pulled into the next rest stop, walked around the car and shook each wheel. The left front wheel had a lot of movement. I opened my trunk, took out the lug wrench and removed the hubcap. Of the five studs, only three of them had lug nuts and those were loose enough to turn by hand. The other two were missing altogether. I had just changed this tire three weeks before and knew I put all five lug nuts back on. There's no way I could have left two of them off, and they weren't rolling around inside the hubcap. They were missing, plain and simple.

My mind quickly flashed back to the incident at the recruiting section when my brake line was cut. It had happened again. I tightened up the three lug nuts that were loose and took one from one of the other wheels to replace one of the missing ones. I sat in the rest stop a few more minutes digesting what had just occurred before continuing my slow ride back to Detroit. I recorded the incident in my diary that night and reviewed other incidents that had occurred since I had begun to keeping it. Very few of the entries were positive. The following morning, after Lola had left for work, I drove out to Palmer Park, a place I often went to unwind. I sat on top one of the picnic tables and went over everything that had happened to me since joining the force.

"Why am I still here? Why do I keep taking all of this shit? How can so many people dislike one person so much? I'm a nice guy, I like helping people, I'm friendly, I keep a smile on my face most of the time, and laugh and tell silly jokes with everybody, even strangers. Why am I going through all of this?"

Before I could answer myself, a visitor to the park, just a random stranger, interrupted my thoughts with a question. I got back in my car and drove home.

I got another good night's sleep and after three more days of vacation, I returned to work. While I was gone, Jack had somehow managed to get off the car. We were no longer

114

partners. I wasn't the least bit disappointed. However, my new partner was no better than Jack. I approached the lieutenant and asked if I could work inside whenever there was a vacancy. I also asked to be permanently assigned to a one-man car if one became available. Most patrol cars in Detroit have two officers, cars that only take reports and handle accidents have just one officer. Both of my requests were granted

The sergeant's exam was coming up and with four years on the job, I was now eligible to take it. Working inside, taking walk in reports, and working a one man car gave me a lot of free time and a chance to study for the exam. I passed all phases of the sergeant's exam and made the promotion list.

Some of my old arrests were coming up for trial and I often had to appear in court. At one of my court appearances I ran into Richard, Louise's boyfriend and the one who was making all the threats against my life and other members of Detail 318. He admitted to me that he hated the task force lieutenant and threatened to kill him. When I asked him if I was on his hit list, he ignored the question.

Six months had now passed since the death of Lola's father. The situation between she and I had gotten to the point that we hardly talked to one another. All forms of intimacy and affection had completely disappeared from the marriage. We were simply two people sharing the same household with a five-year-old daughter. One weekend Lola went to visit her mother; I took this opportunity to move out of our apartment and into one of my own. This was without doubt the most cowardly act of my life. I left like a thief in the night, but I just couldn't stay any longer.

Lola minced no words in denouncing this despicable act, and she was right. What little respect she had for me was now completely gone. After things cooled down, we began to talk again. In fact, we did a little more than just talk, but it was not enough to make me go back home.

During this time of separation, Lola's mother became gravely ill. The doctors gave her about a year to live, which turned out to be a generous estimate. She died a few months after being diagnosed. It had only been ten months since Lola had lost her father to a heart attack; now, she's lost her mother to cancer. And, as if that weren't enough, she also learned she was pregnant with our second child. I knew what I was supposed to do, but I wasn't sure if it was the right decision, but guilt is a heavy load. If Lola ever needed a shoulder to lean on, it was now. At the end of the month I moved out of my apartment and back in with Lola.

Me & two of New York's finest

Once a Cop – Always a Cop

Chapter Eight
Meet the Sergeant

W hen I reported to work a few days later, I was called into the lieutenant's office.

"What have I done now?'

"Well Crawford, you have had a very interesting but shaky stay here at the precinct. All of that is about to come to an end.

"Oh shit!'"

"I have been notified that you are to report to the police academy on Monday to begin officer's candidate school. Let me be the first to congratulate you, Sergeant Crawford."

I literally ran back to the detective bureau to tell my good friend Johnnie.

"J.T., I would like you to meet Sergeant James Edward Crawford of the Detroit Police Department!"

"Sergeant James Edward Crawford, I would like you to meet Sergeant Johnnie Thomas of the Detroit Police Department!"

"What, You too?"

"Yes, me, too. You're not the only one who passed the exam."

We were as excited as two young kids and we acted like it.

By now several officers and supervisors had gathered. One of them was a white sergeant with over thirty five years on the job. He tried his best to burst our bubble, but we weren't having it.

"I don't know what you two are so goddamn happy about? You sure as hell didn't earn it."

"And what the hell is that supposed to mean?" asked J.T.

"You know damn well what it means. With the new black mayor and his Affirmative Action program, I guess you two will be inspectors by next year. I think it is a damn shame that they skipped over all of those qualified white boys to get to you two. It isn't fair and you both know it."

Johnnie started going off on him. I stopped him. We literally laughed in his face, up close and personal. That was enough satisfaction for us. The white sergeant who blasted J.T. and me about our promotions was only one of hundreds who felt the same way but weren't quite so vocal. Detroit had just elected its first black mayor, Coleman Young, and he implemented an Affirmative Action program in the police department to help level the playing field.

Promotion to the rank of sergeant and lieutenant are determined by a competitive exam, an oral exam, performance evaluation rating, college credits, and credit for being in the military. All appointments above the rank of lieutenant, which include the rank of inspector, commander, deputy chief, executive deputy chief and chief, are made at the pleasure of the mayor. When Young came into office the 5400-man force was top heavy with white supervisors, especially in the high command ranks. There were only a smattering of black lieutenants and a slightly larger number of black sergeants. Only a handful is promoted off each list, sergeants and lieutenants, annually.

The biggest discrepancy and obstacle for the black officer came from the performance evaluation ratings or service ratings as they were called. They were one-hundred percent subjective, and blacks were always near the bottom. Technically a rating of one-hundred was possible; however ninety was usually the highest score anyone ever received. The majority of the white officers had ratings in the mid to high eighties or ninety. The black officers were mostly in the low eighties, seventies, and high sixties. A five or six point higher service rating could move an officer up several positions on the promotion list.

With the old system of promoting, once an officer made the promotion list the chief could promote him or her regardless of their position on the list. If he wanted to, the chief could go down to the very bottom of the list and pick one of his favorites or others that he or someone else wanted promoted. That practice was later abandoned and promotions, in most instances, were made strictly in numerical order. Young went back to the old system and that created havoc.

His new policy was that for every white officer that was promoted from the list, a black officer, a female and other minorities such as Hispanics, Asian, and Native American also had to be promoted. That meant that the first black officer who may have been twentieth on the list would get promoted before the second white officer who was number two on the list.

From the outside looking in, that was wrong as hell. However, if black officers had not been given such low service ratings and low scores on their equally subjective oral interviews, they would have appeared much higher on the promotion lists. It was discrimination that kept black officers from being promoted earlier and discrimination that promoted them later. I see that as a tie.

I was told that Satchel Paige used to pitch double headers. If he, Jackie Robinson, Josh Gibson and other black players had been allowed to play in the major leagues, would Babe Ruth, Ted Williams and other white players have held the records they did? I don't think so. Look what happened when black college quarterbacks were finally allowed to play their positions in the NFL instead of being relegated to wide receivers because they did not have the "necessities" to be quarterbacks in the NFL. Can we say Doug Williams, Warren Moon, Randall Cunningham, Russell Wilson and Cam Newton? And, look what happened when they stopped recycling fired white coaches in the NFL and started hiring qualified black ones, can we say Super Bowl 41, Lovie Smith against Tony Dungy, and Mike Tomlison in Pittsburgh?

Affirmative Action divided the officers of all ranks like no other issue in the history of the Detroit Police Department. Racism had raised its ugly head and battle lines were drawn. Those unhappy with the department and Affirmative Action were determined to bring it to its knees. Ten years after I joined the department and six years after the mayor was elected, the unions were still fighting his Affirmative Action promotions.

In one of the cases I was actually named as an intervening defendant. They wanted to rescind my promotion.

BAKER v. CITY OF DETROIT
United States District Court, E. D. Michigan, S. D.
November 17, 1980.

Kenneth BAKER, Arthur Bartniczak, Hanson Bratton, Patrick Jordan, Frank Krezowik, Elbert McVay and Robert Scally, Plaintiffs, and Hanson Bratton, Gale Bogenn, William Shell, Patrick Jordan, Charles Mahoney, Individually and on behalf of all others similarly situated and The Detroit Police Lieutenants & Sergeants Association, Plaintiffs, v. CITY OF DETROIT, a Municipal corporation; Philip G. Tannian, Chief of Police; Coleman A. Young, Mayor, City of Detroit; and The Board of Police Commissioners, City of Detroit, Defendants, and Guardians of Michigan, David L. Simmons, Arnold D. Payne, *James E. Crawford,* Clinton Donaldson, Willie Johnson, Kenneth M. Johnson and Alfred Brooks, Intervening Defendants. Despite all of the controversy and tension, Affirmative Action promotions continued and because of it I was headed to class to become a sergeant.

122

"You are working the midnight shift. At 3:30 a.m. one of your crew gets a police run on a burglary in progress. The dispatcher calls them several times, but gets no response. After trying unsuccessfully for ten minutes to reach the crew, the dispatcher finally assigns the police run to someone else. You, the sergeant, are notified that you have a crew that has failed to respond to a police run. You are given their last location and told to find their whereabouts. Having worked that precinct as a patrolman, you know where all the sleeping holes are and head for the nearest one. Sure as hell, you find the crew, sound asleep. One of them is your best friend and the other is your ex-partner.

"What do you do, sergeant?"

"Sir, I would ask them if their wife is working, because their next paycheck is going to be a few dollars short."

The entire classroom laughed.

"What about you, sergeant?"

"I would notify the dispatcher that I found the crew and that they were okay. Then, I'd handle the situation with the officers."

"What does that mean; you'll handle the situation? Remember, they have just missed a priority one police run. The dispatcher is required to make written notification to his boss who in turn will make written notification to your boss. Your boss is going to want an investigation and a recommendation from you on possible disciplinary action. Also remember this is your best friend and ex-partner you just caught sleeping. What do you do?"

"I would tell the officers that they knew when they pulled into the hole it was against the rules and that I have no choice but to recommend disciplinary action."

"But wait a minute, sergeant, the crew says to you, "Hey buddy, a few weeks ago you were doing the same thing yourself. How are you going to burn us?" What do say to that?"

123

"I'd say that I wasn't a sergeant then and now I am. I have no choice. I have to do something."

"And, how do you respond when they say, "Oh, I see, it was okay a few weeks ago but now that you are a big time sergeant you have to turn us in?""

The class was clueless as to what to say next. There was no right or wrong answer.

"Gentlemen, and ladies, this is only one of many situations you will be facing after leaving this classroom. You will no longer be one of the fellows. You will now be a part of supervision. The transformation from police officer to sergeant will be the most difficult transition you will face in your career. How you handle it initially may well determine whether or not you will succeed as a supervisor. It may also determine whether or not you will continue to move up the supervisory ladder. In addition to dealing with your friends, many of you, for the first time in your life, may end up working for a black boss. And, let me tell you right now, you better get used to it, because it is a sign of things to come to this department."

It was obvious that many of the officers were very uneasy about some of the things we were hearing, and the scenarios that had just been presented. Most of us had never seriously considered the problems we might have with our friends, nor the racial aspects associated with having a black boss. Each candidate knew becoming a sergeant would mean more responsibilities and entail making critical decisions, but none of us had really stopped to seriously think about the changes that would take place in both our personal and professional lives.

"Some of you will be able to handle these situations and will go on to become good supervisors. Others of you won't be able to separate yourselves from the good ol' boys network and will become poor and ineffective supervisors. The officers will constantly test you. If they find a weakness, they'll exploit it and pass the word around. You will either earn their respect or you will become the precinct joke. Therefore, it is so important that when you are forced into a position where a decision has to be made, that you make some type of decision. Always remember, a bad decision is better than no decision at all. Second, you must be firm in whatever decision you make. And third, you must be prepared to defend that decision."

I did not necessarily agree with the statement that a bad decision is better than none at all, but he sure opened my eyes. Following our three weeks of training, a graduation ceremony was held and we were presented our badges. As my name was called and I walked across that stage to receive it from the chief, I experienced the greatest feeling I had had since receiving my bachelor's degree. All of the aggravation I had experienced over the past four years seemed irrelevant and obscure. As the chief and I stood face to face, he could see the elation in my face.

"It's a wonderful feeling, isn't it sergeant?"

"Yes, Sir, it certainly is."

Sergeant James Edward Crawford

125

After the picture-taking and coffee and cake were over, we were given our first assignments. Mine was the Fourth Precinct. It was one of the smallest precincts in the city, had a relatively low crime rate and was heavily Hispanic. It wasn't bad for a first assignment. Graduation was on Friday; the new assignments began on Monday. However, for me it began Sunday night at 10:30 p. m. when I reported for duty. I had drawn the midnight shift.

I was so nervous I didn't know what to do. My mind was racing all over the place. "What if they ask me a question I couldn't answer? What if I have a barricaded gunman or something like that. What if my first decision is the wrong decision? Do I act tough like I really know what I am doing, or do I act like a new sergeant who's just learning?"

I was greeted with mixed reactions from my new colleagues. No one was rude, but everyone had strong opinions on the new Affirmative Action promotions that were taking place and they did not mind expressing them.

The shift was less than three hours old when I was called to a scene and had to make my first supervisory decision. It involved some officers who wanted to have the fire department come out and let them go upon the roof with one of their ladders so they could catch some burglars who had gotten up there the same way, and pulled their latter up behind them. A passerby had witnessed them going onto the roof. I said no and told them to wait for the owner to come from home. They weren't too happy with my decision. They were anxious to get inside and corner the bad guys. It was also more macho to go up the ladder to catch the crooks rather than walk through the front door. The owner arrived and the bad guys were taken into custody.

I had now made my first decision as a supervisor. I reviewed that decision over and over in my mind during the night. After that, the decisions came fast and furious. Most of them were minor. However, I knew it wouldn't be long

126

before the big one to come, and it did a few weeks later when officers were chasing a stolen car and the occupant jumped out and began running between the houses. They opened fire on him, a definite no-no in the Detroit Police Department.

By the time I arrived, the driver was in custody.

"Who fired the shots?"

No one answered. I asked again in a slow and stern voice.

"Who fired the shots?"

The officers looked at each other. No one said a word. I then approached each officer individually and asked if he had fired a shot. They all denied firing a shot.

"Gentlemen, let's not make this worse than it is. One of you or several of you fired a shot. We have it on tape. I will give all of you thirty seconds to decide what you want to do and then I'll decide what I have to do. Okay?"

I took the prisoner aside and positioned myself between the officers and the prisoner so they could not hear what I was saying. I also kept a close eye on the officers, frequently looking back to make sure none of them left or tried to leave or reload their weapon. After a few seconds three officers stepped forward and admitted they had fired their weapon at the suspect.

"You know you cannot fire at a car thief unless he fires at you or your life is in danger, right?"

All of the officers nodded their heads.

"So, then why did you shoot?"

"Sarge, I saw something shiny in his hand. I thought he had a weapon."

"You thought he had a weapon, but you did not actually see a weapon, right?"

"No, Sir, I didn't."

"All three of you saw the shiny object at the same time, right, and that's why all three of you shot?" No one responded.

127

We now have gone to Chapter Two of the "Handbook", the ubiquitous shiny object which always appears when the officer knowingly fires his weapon when he shouldn't have. They knew I did not believe a word they were saying, and I knew they were not going to change their story. I confiscated their weapons as required and ordered them to head to the precinct to make their reports. To cover my ass, I had other officers to check the area for the alleged shiny object. None was found.

As I was going through my transition from police officer to sergeant, the mayor decided to restructure the department. He replaced the rank of commissioner and appointed a white chief of police. The assistant commissioner was replaced with a black executive deputy chief. The city was divided into five sections and a deputy chief was appointed to each section. When the dust settled we had three black deputy chiefs, one white deputy chief, and one deputy chief of Middle Eastern descent.

DETROIT POLICE

Certificate of Promotion

Know all men by these presents that

JAMES E. CRAWFORD

is promoted to the rank of

SERGEANT

in the DETROIT POLICE DEPARTMENT

and is charged with the duties and responsibilities and shall have the authority conferred upon one in his rank and assignment.

This promotion is officially recorded in General Order #74-298 Personnel effective October 11, 1974.

IN TESTIMONY WHEREOF, I have hereunto placed my signature and caused the Seal of the Detroit Police Department to be affixed at Detroit, Michigan, this 28th day of October in the year of our Lord one thousand nine hundred and seventy-five,

_____ *Commissioner*

J.P.D. 446

C of D—89-CE (5-6)

Once a Cop – Always a Cop

Chapter Nine
Disasters by the Numbers

L ess than three months after being assigned to the Fourth Precinct, I was called into the commander's office. I wasn't sure what to expect.

"Well, Crawford, apparently the big wigs downtown think you are a pretty important guy."

"Why is that, sir?"

"I just got a call from the office of the new executive deputy chief. He has personally chosen you to be on his staff. "Must be nice?"

The new EDC was Frank, the precinct commander who had befriended me when I left the task force and went to the Thirteenth Precinct. I wasn't sure if I should jump for joy or not. The last time I was hand-picked by the third floor I ended up on Detail 318. I had no idea what to expect on this new assignment and really didn't care. I decided to go in with an open mind and not anticipate the worse. I spent the weekend relaxing, watching football, and playing with Tracey. The DPD was the last thing on my mind.

I reported to my new post the following Monday. Ben, who was a lieutenant, and Stanley, Robert and Gene, all sergeants, also reported. One of the EDC's other staff members was my old friend Vivian from recruiting. I had seen the others before but did not know them personally. The lieutenant called us aside and gave a short briefing. I did not like what I heard. We then went in to meet with the EDC.

With the new command structure being put in place, the EDC wanted all of the precincts to be operating at the same level, maintaining the same log books, processing prisoners and property the same way, and wanted more accountability from his street supervisors. We, the new inspection team, were to make sure this happened. Our job was to audit all of the record books at each precinct and have them brought up to date. We were to check for cleanliness at the stations, monitor police runs to see how quickly the officers were responding, and monitor the decisions of the responding supervisors. We were not to take any action or give any orders unless it was a life or death situation.

You got this; one lieutenant and four sergeants were going to be looking over the shoulders of commanders, inspectors, lieutenants, and other sergeants to see how well they are doing their jobs.

Why me? Why couldn't they have picked Walter Kaminski or Roosevelt Jones? This was the last thing I needed. And you can imagine how well we were received. I needed this assignment like I needed a hole in the head. Before the inspection team became fully operational, we went to each precinct and briefed the commander. We would select a precinct, in no special order, and then spend several days there doing our audits. Any deficiencies had to be corrected within thirty days.

In almost every precinct the area that was in the worst shape was the property room. Each precinct had its own property room, with the main one being downtown. We found property listed in the book as being at the main property room downtown, sitting on shelves at the precinct, including narcotics, which are supposed to go downtown immediately after the arrest. There was also property missing altogether and property on the shelves at the precinct that was not listed in any book, anywhere.

132

When monitoring the police runs, often we were closer to the location of the run than the responding officers and got there first. The officers accused us of calling in false runs and waiting to see how long it took for them to respond. The responding supervisors felt we were usurping their authority by looking over their shoulder, and rightfully so. It was not a good situation. My former stint on Detail 318 and now this assignment to the inspection team did not help my image one bit. I hated it already. I had just begun my thirty third year in life, but after all I had gone through the last four years, I felt like I was in my early hundreds.

A week before Christmas my close friend, Martin, whom I had gone to high school with and graduated with, was killed. He was standing on the wing of his small airplane when he slipped on the ice, lost his balance, and was struck by the propeller. He died instantly. I had known his wife Claudia since elementary school. Upon learning of his death I went by to see her. After things settled down I began to spend more and more time with her. This was another instance in my life where timing was not my friend, especially when it related to romance.

I have always had inconsistencies in my life, but one area where I was very consistent was when I made the decision to end a relationship. Sometimes I may have given it a second try, but in the end, I stuck to my original decision to end it. That was the case when I decided to go back home. I knew that once Lola had our second child, got back on her feet, and went back to work, I was outta there. Many thought that to be cold and that I shouldn't have gone back in the first place. They may have been right.

A few months after we got back together, our second child, Theresa, was born. I met with some of my old classmates from 70K at a local bar, passed out cigars, and left feeling pretty good. Had I been stopped, I'm not sure if I could have passed the field sobriety test. I'm not a drinker by any stretch of the imagination. After one beer, I get sleepy as hell, and don't let me have a couple of drinks.

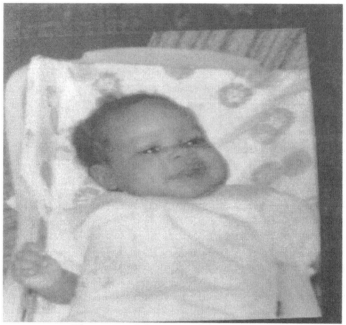

Theresa – My second born

The loss of Martin was devastating for Claudia, as expected. He was her first love, and for quite a while she refused to accept his death, choosing to believe that one day he was going to walk through the door again and that she would wake up from the awful dream she was having. I was her shoulder to cry on. Big mistake! It all started out very innocently and I was just going there as a friend. I even asked Lola to come with me. However, things escalated. Lola noticed the change in my behavior right away. This began the final stage of the dissolution of our marriage.

One evening I was tired and fell asleep on Claudia's couch. She purposely didn't bother to wake me up. Claudia knew that not waking me up was wrong, but she did not care. I was helping to ease her pain and that's all she cared about. When I finally woke up, it was nearly midnight. I was pissed. When I got home, Lola was waiting for me. She had driven by Claudia's house and saw my car. I have never done anything like this before, ever. Later that day as I was taking a bath before going to work, Lola walked in and just stood there a few seconds, leaning against the door frame. I could see the hurt in her face.

"You know, I feel like blowing your balls off."

She did not have a weapon in her hand, but my three guns were less than fifty feet away, and I had to get past her to get to them. I must have set a record for a man getting out of a bathtub. I moved out a short time later. Our divorce became final soon after. As time passed, getting married again was simply out of the question. If anyone I dated even mentioned the word marriage, I was gone. I was determined to never, ever do this again. I have often been asked why I was so adamant about not getting married again.

I have three short answers, and they probably don't make sense to anyone but me. First, I felt that if I couldn't raise my own children in my house, I wasn't going to raise anyone else's in my house. Nearly every woman I dated had children. And if I married one of them, and I am feeding, clothing, spending quality and quantity time with them, and spending my money on them, and then one of those little darlings doesn't get his or her way, or when I tell them to do something and he yells, "You ain't my daddy" his ass was gone home to his daddy. And if the momma had a problem with that, she was gone too. That meant the possibility of a second failed marriage, my greatest fear.

Second, I listened to folks all the time talking about their first wife, first husband, my second wife, my second husband; I just didn't want to ever be able to say that. I wanted just one marriage and I wanted it to last until one of

135

us died, just like my parents who were married forty-seven years before my dad passed away.

Third, after I retired most of the women I was dating were still working and they couldn't always get the time off to travel with me and I had plenty of places I wanted to go. That was a handicap for me. If I decided to just get up and go somewhere for a day, week, or month, I did not want to ask permission or wait until my girlfriend was on vacation. And, there were times when I simply wanted to go by myself. You cannot do these things if you are married.

After my divorce and subsequent break up with Claudia, I went back to my Kettering days where no woman with a pulse and a heart beat was safe. My good friend Vivian and I had several heated arguments about my consorting and carousing with some of the female officers on the job, especially those at my precinct. It wasn't against the rules; they were all single, I was single, and they received no special favors, at least not at work. To say that I was on the rebound would be an understatement.

While our inspection team was conducting an inspection at one of the precincts, a department wide teletype came out stating that my former partner from Number 10, Maurice, was in the hospital in critical condition. I went there right away. The nurse told me that Maurice was clinically dead and they were just waiting for his wife to make the decision to shut off the ventilator so they could harvest his organs.

Maurice and I had not spoken since I left Detail 318. I stepped closer to his bed. Maurice was hooked up to a breathing machine which was caused his stomach to move in and out. There was no other body movement whatsoever. I was angry, mainly with him, but also at the lieutenant, George, who convinced him to join the task force in the first place. I lashed out as he lay there, dying.

"Why didn't you quit when I did? Why was this so damn important to you? Just two years ago you told me that you were going to live to be the oldest man in the world, and now look at you. You're only twenty –nine, and your body is lifeless. You won't even know the final results of the investigation you worked on so long and hard. And for what, Maurice, for what? I stood there for several more minutes. Then I patted him on the hand, and then walked out.

Maurice had been at a motel guarding some witnesses when he fell down a flight of steps and struck his head. He died from a fractured skull. The official report said that a stroke may have caused him to fall. A stroke at age twenty-nine? Maurice's family argued that either the officers he was investigating murdered him or it was the mob. The chief didn't help matters when he told the media that there were many unanswered questions about Maurice's death. The story captured the newspaper headlines and the local television news for weeks.

After Detail 318 ended, one member from the Attorney General's office, Walt, also died. He was in his forties and had a heart attack.

137

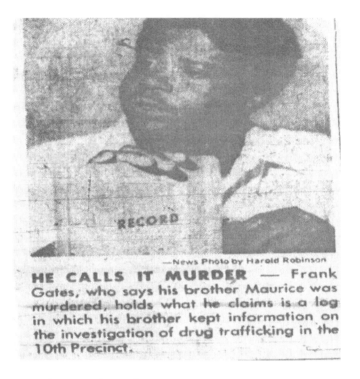

—News Photo by Harold Robinson

HE CALLS IT MURDER — Frank Gates, who says his brother Maurice was murdered, holds what he claims is a log in which his brother kept information on the investigation of drug trafficking in the 10th Precinct.

Maurice's and my former partner at Number 10, Ron, who had joined the task force after I left, also suffered a stroke, but did not die. He was also in his forties. Then there was Melvin, our sergeant on Detail 318; he suffers from severe migraine headaches. It looks like leaving the task force was one of my better decisions.

Other newspaper articles had been critical of the task force and all the money it had spent so far. Many also questioned the character of some of the key witnesses, like Shooter.

It was later learned that the key witness for Detail 318, a dope dealer who was allegedly paying off the officers, was wanted for murder in Alabama, and the lieutenant knew it. Two other informants that I had arrested earlier in my career

138

and who came aboard after I left the task force, got into a fight. One of them killed the other, wrapped him in a rug, and dumped him in the woods. Another witness admitted on the stand that he had been paid for his testimony. When all was said and done, somehow three police officers and four civilians were convicted and sentenced to prison. The operation cost millions.

The birth of my second daughter was about the only good thing that happened so far during this thirty-third year.

A month after Maurice's death, I got a call from my family to get to Grand Rapids as soon as I could. It was my father. He was suffering from lung cancer and had taken a turn for the worse. When I got to the hospital my brothers Alan, Bobby and Donald were there as well as my mother and my sister-n-law, Gwen. My father was going in and out of consciousness. We all gathered around his bed. He was lying on his left side, facing the wall when my mother said to him "Jimmy is here."

He turned his head toward us, his eyes opened wide, and then he looked straight up at me. Without saying a word, he closed his eyes and turned back toward the wall. It was the most eerie feeling I'd ever experienced. Our Episcopal priest came in and offered a prayer. It was short and he said something I had never heard any man of God say.

"God, either take away Malvern's pain and suffering or let him go."

We all left and went to the waiting room. As we sat there trying to figure out what to do next, my mother suddenly jumped up and walked out. She returned a few minutes later.

"He's gone."

That prayer by Father Stephens haunted me for weeks. He told God to stop my father's pain or take him away, and he did. My father was eighty-one years old.

My Dad and Me

140

I wish I had had a better relationship with my father as did my siblings. It is difficult for those growing up in this "now" generation to understand the relationships we had with our parents in the "then" generation. It was so different. We had no doubt that our parents loved us, but the affection we see expressed today, hugs, kisses, men embracing one another, "I love you" at the end of conversations, was practically nonexistent in the forties, fifties, and sixties. It was almost as though our parents were afraid to show affection, especially the men.

As our kids became teenagers and young adults, that has changed. But; it was not an easy transition for us old timers. I still struggle with it today.

After moving to Detroit, my relationship with Roy, my best friend during childhood, weaned somewhat. Our lives took different paths, and we often found ourselves on opposite sides of the law, something we laughed about whenever we did get together. Although we kept in contact with one another, it was not the same as it was in the past. However, my relationship with another friend, Joe, grew steadily. As it had been with Roy and me during our childhood, as adults, Joe and I were very close. When I still lived in Grand Rapids, if you saw Joe, you knew I was somewhere around.

After I moved to Detroit we visited back and forth as often as we could. One summer, when I was still in college, he and I worked the midnight shift at one of the hospitals. Jessie, our supervisor, couldn't stay awake and could often be found sleeping under one of the pews in the chapel. After a while, when Joe and I finished our work, we did the same thing.

We just made sure that Jessie wasn't around. One night he walked in and caught us sleeping.

"As long as you two are asleep you got your job, but when you wake up, you're fired!"

We had all we could do not to laugh, and we didn't open our eyes until he left the room. We slipped out and went to work immediately, making sure he saw us. When he tried to threaten us again, we reminded him that we were only doing what we saw him doing every night. He told us not to do it again. We didn't.

When I moved to Detroit and became a cop, Joe was already a county sheriff in Grand Rapids. Whenever I came to town, we hung out the whole time. He and I were only a year apart in age. One summer Joe was diagnosed with cancer. He got weaker with every visit I made. I went to Grand Rapids as often as I could.

Late one evening I got a call from his wife, Sondra, telling me that he was declining fast and that I should get up to Grand Rapids as soon as possible. It was late in the evening and visiting hours were over. I knew it would be close to midnight before I got there so I left early the next morning. I stopped by his house first to get an update on the way to the hospital. As I pulled up, I saw cars parked everywhere. I did not have a good feeling. Sondra opened the door. I could see that she had been crying.

"What's going on?"

"We called, but you had already left. Joe died during the night."

I bolted from the house and began running down the street crying like a baby. Joe's brother, Gene, caught up with me and walked me back to the house. I should have gone to Grand Rapids as soon as I got the call from Sondra and not worried about those stupid ass visiting hours. I'm sure they would have let me in. His family was already at his bedside; I should have been too. I beat myself up for weeks for not going to Grand Rapids that night. That was another negative caused by my follow the rules mentality.

Only a few more months remained in this miserable year, and I couldn't wait for it to come to an end. First it was

Martin, then Maurice, my dad, and now Joe, and, let's not forget the divorce. Wow! And now, I had to go back to Detroit to deal with the bullshit there.

Although life in the department was not very good to me, and although I had gone through all of the deaths, life away from the department was very enjoyable for the most part. That's what kept me going. I spent a lot of time with my girls, taking them to the park, the zoo, and amusement parks, and on short trips: Kings Island in Ohio was our favorite. I attended parent – teacher conferences and attended every event they had since the day they started school. I was there for every award they received. There was no way I was going to let what happened to me, happen to them. I would go by and help them with their homework and rewarded them for good grades. During the weekends that I kept them, they would help me cook, and we played cards and board games. When they moved away to Maryland and I moved to Florida, I never missed a father—daughter day at Theresa's school.

There we played soccer, softball, had the three legged race, and the potato sack race. Some of the other girls' fathers were unable to attend, so I filled in for them when I caught my breath. I loved it, and so did they. Some of my "daughters" were white, some Asian, and Hispanic. I also managed to slip away to Mexico and the Bahamas for two long weekends, and my social life couldn't have been better. Those were the things that kept a smile on my face and allowed me to go to work each day despite what I was going through. I was on a mission with the police department and had a goal to reach. I was determined to prove that officers like Sergeant Gelderblom still existed and, I was going to be one of them.

Once a Cop – Always a Cop

Chapter Ten
The Big Shake Up

As I headed back to Detroit and the inspection team, the last thing I needed was more aggravation from disgruntled police officers and supervisors we were monitoring. However, a new problem had erupted that absolutely had nothing to do with me personally. Thank God. Tension between the mayor and the top two executives in the police department was growing after a rumor surfaced that the current chief was going to be ousted and replaced by my boss, Frank, the EDC. A second rumor also surfaced stating that Frank was involved in drugs with his long time friend, Leo. Sources said that the chief, a former FBI agent, believed that his ouster was imminent and many believed he started the rumor about Frank in order to save his job.

Anyone who knew Frank knew there was absolutely no truth to the accusation. Next to me, he was probably the last person in Detroit to get involved with drugs. But that didn't stop the chief from setting up surveillance on Frank and his entire staff, including me. Frank's office was bugged, Leo's trailer was bugged, and our cars and home phones were bugged. Due to this battle, the inspection team was put on hold, Frank was placed on sick leave, and the three of the four sergeants, Stanley, Robert and me were assigned as Frank's personal bodyguards.

The more this fiasco went on the angrier Frank got, the more he drank, and the more paranoid he became. He thought that everyone was out to get him, including me. Yes, me. He called us all together for a meeting at his house. He was as angry as I had ever seen him.

145

"I gotta call saying that someone on my staff was working with the chief to help bring me down."

I never believed that statement. We all looked at each other, wondering who it could be. At this time I think the liquor was talking more than him. He then pointed his finger at me.

"You, motherfucker, are the one I know the least. And you worked that bullshit detail with George. I think it's you."

My jaws dropped. I could not believe what I was hearing. He then went on to challenge my loyalty to him and belittled me before the entire staff. I just sat there and took it. I said very little during his tirade, and believe me it was brutal. He even admitted to having me followed. I could see that everyone was uneasy, but no one bothered to intervene. I guess their thinking was that if I didn't say something, why should they.

Later that night I received a telephone call from one of our civilian staffers, Julie, who had attended that meeting. She was several years older than me and had worked for Frank for years.

"Crawford, why did you just sit there and take that brutal attack from Frank? Even I was embarrassed. You are a grown man just like he is. You need to start acting like one."

She slammed the phone done in my ear. I was already feeling like a wimp; this certainly didn't help.

In a popular television show from the early eighties called, *Hill Street Blues,* the head of a fictitious squad of police officers was Captain Frank Furillo. Furillo was a rough and tough man who had the answers for everything and backed his men all the way to the wall. He was the ideal boss. The show came on the air after I worked for Frank, but they were one and the same. Furillo was the closest person I could compare to Frank.

I saw Frank as my Captain Furillo and I greatly admired him. I often thought that if I ever got to his rank, EDC or

146

even my dream of commander, I wanted to be just like him. To see him and his reputation being ruined by lies and innuendos, his ever-rising use of alcohol, and frequent breakdown to tears, was hard to take. It was like watching a hero go down in flames. I suspect that is why I didn't tell him to go to hell during his tirade, or maybe I was just afraid to challenge him. I can be a wimp at times.

Everything came to a head when the chief, along with his former FBI buddies, raided Frank's home looking for drugs. Of course they did not find any. Frank and all of us bodyguards were out on a boat when the raid took place. The chief knew that, and went so far as to have Frank's office staff placed under house arrest while the raid went on. They were not allowed to leave the office or to make or answer any telephone calls. Frank was totally unaware of what he was about to face when he got home. We, the bodyguards, went to the office from the boat where we too were placed under house arrest until the raid was over.

The story made national headlines and Detroit again became the laughing stock of the nation. First there was the raid on the Tenth Precinct and now you have the chief of police raiding the home of his second in command looking for drugs. In my wildest dream I never thought that I would see anything like this. I had been looking at being a police officer through rose colored glasses. That dream I had as an eight year old was beginning to shatter.

The mayor fired the chief and allowed Frank to retire.

Before he left, he called in his staff and thanked all of us for our loyalty, including me. He said that he had asked the mayor to promote everyone on his immediate staff to the rank of inspector or above if they weren't already an inspector. He said the mayor agreed. There were five of us on his immediate staff. Three became commanders, one became an inspector, and Stanley rose to become chief of police. Before

147

leaving his office Frank asked me to stay for a man-to-man talk.

"What the fuck is wrong with us? Why can't we get along?"

"I don't know. I guess it's because you don't trust me."

That's part of it. The fact that you worked for that son-of-a- bitch, George, on that task force has a lot to do with it."

"Working for him was one of the biggest mistakes I've made since joining this sorry ass police department. Working for him will haunt me as long as I am on this job, and there is absolutely nothing I can do to change that."

"To be honest, one of the reasons I have been so hard on you is because you remind me so much of myself. We are both fighters and we are both willing to go to the wall for what we believe in. That's a rare quality these days, especially in this department. When I look at you and what you've been trying to do, the changes you are trying to make, and I see all the shit you have taken, I'm seeing myself twenty years ago, a young dumb ass cop who thought that he was going to come in and make a difference."

"But you have made a difference. That's why I am glad I came to work for you. It hasn't been easy watching how they have treated you. If they can do this to you, the executive deputy chief, what chance do I have?"

Frank was second in command of The Detroit Police Department, and Barack Obama is the first in command of the entire free world. One would never know it by the way both have been treated. I have the utmost respect for both of them, and it has been difficult watching both of them being torn apart and disrespected.

Frank and I talked a few more minutes. The meeting ended with an embrace and a firm handshake.

When I wrote my book, *Officer in Trouble,* I used a term to describe Frank and his drinking that was not very

148

flattering. It is a term I regret ever using. In retrospect, I would also have been offended if I were him. He and I talked about the comment after my book was published. He was very angry with me, as was his son Michael. I apologized to him profusely, but to no avail. I could not call the bullet back, nor could I unring the bell. All I could do was offer an apology. Twenty-four years later I again offer that same apology to Mike.

In that same paragraph where I used that term, I also talked about how much I admired and respected Frank, and that if I ever reach his rank, I would like to be just like him. However, it wasn't enough to curb their anger.

Bethune – Cookman Department of
Public Safety
Once a Cop – Always a Cop

Chapter Eleven
The Paper Tiger

After leaving the EDC's office, my new assignment took me to the Eleventh Precinct. I had visited there while I was on the inspection team, but other than that, I wasn't really too familiar with it. I did have one small advantage. My new inspector, Big John, and Frank were best friends and had been for over twenty-five years. On the very first day one of my fellow sergeants made a comment about my tour of duty with Detail 318, but other than that, my presence didn't seem to be a big deal.

Midway through the year, the department gave its annual exam for the rank of lieutenant. I passed the written test, the oral exam, had the maximum performance evaluation rating that could be given and I got points for my college degree. I made the new lieutenant's list. The department had a policy of promoting each year just before Christmas and I was hoping that the policy wouldn't change this year. It didn't. A month before Christmas I was officially notified to report to the police academy for officers' candidate school for the rank of lieutenant.

Four weeks later, Sergeant James Edward Crawford became Lieutenant James Edward Crawford. There were four other sergeants from the 11th precinct to make lieutenant. In an unusual move, none of us from the graduating class was assigned to a new location until eight days after graduation. All five of us went back to Number 11, which made the precinct top heavy in lieutenants. I went from assisting the shift lieutenant to being the shift lieutenant. My boss was no longer "sir" he was Andy. We went from wearing blue shirts with chevrons to white shirts with gold bars. That took some getting used to. My fear of making the wrong decision no longer haunted me as it had when I first made sergeant. And, my confidence was high as ever after three years of being a supervisor.

Our new assignments were finally made. I was sent back to the 13th precinct. It was the first place I went after leaving Detail 318. I was now Fat Jack's boss instead of his partner. The officers who called in sick rather than work with me were now two grades below me. The sergeants who put me through hell were now addressing me as "sir." I'm certain they were gritting their teeth every time they had to say it. It is kinda like Boehner and McConnell having to say, "Mr. President."

My mother always told me to treat people as you want to be treated because the same people you pass on the way up, you may need on the way down. Many of them at Number 13 had not treated me well. There was one officer in particular, Robert, who was my partner for three months when I was a patrolman. At that time he had been on the force for over ten years and was a know it all. He thought he was the best cop in Detroit. He never called me by my name; it was always "asshole." "Asshole, fill up the car. Asshole, get the vests. Asshole, write the report."

He thought it was funny. He had a smile on his face each time he said it. I ignored in the beginning, but after a short time with the "asshole" treatment, he often became the recipient of my middle finger. Robert was now one of my sergeants. Upon my return to Number 13, and after he was assigned to my shift, he was nervous as hell. Even when we were alone, he sweated bullets and "Yes Sir-ed" the hell out of me.

"Bob. Bob. There's no one in this room but you and me, okay?"

"Yes, sir."

152

I just shook my head. I didn't have a problem with old partners and other friends on the department calling me by my first name. Most of them respected my rank when others were around.

My new boss, the precinct commander, was my old lieutenant from Number 10, the one who did not believe me when I said I did not beat the prisoners. I was hoping he had a short memory; it had been almost seven years since the incident. Ronald was the patrol inspector and the person to whom I had to report. Even though Ronald had never met me, when he learned I was coming, he submitted a request to the deputy chief of our district asking that I be assigned somewhere else. His request was denied.

Ronald called his new lieutenants in for a general briefing and then talked to us individually before giving us our new assignments. When I was called in he wasted no time in letting me know that I was not welcome at the precinct. This was my second stint there and both started out the same. The first time it was Fat Jack; now it was Ronald's turn.

"I've never met you personally, Lieutenant, but from what I have heard, you aren't wanted here and you don't belong here. And; if I have my way about it, you won't be here very long."

Before I could respond to his opening remarks, he hit me with a second cold blast.

"The department has seen fit to make you a lieutenant through its Affirmative Action program and I have no choice but to accept that. I am going to watch you carefully and if you screw up just once, you're out of here."

I was speechless. There was absolutely nothing I could say in response to his blistering. I was a thirty-five year old lieutenant on the nation's fifth largest police department, not a cadet in the academy. *Daaaaaaaaaaaaayum!*

153

Lieutenant James Edward Crawford

Ronald wasted no time in keeping his promise to drive me from the precinct. Having three vacancies for shift lieutenants, and with me having the most experience working the shifts as a sergeant, I felt certain I would be given one of them. That did not happen. Instead, I was made the relief lieutenant, which meant I bounce from shift to shift, filling in for the regular lieutenant when he/she was on leave. The day shift was from 8:00 AM. to 4:00 PM, afternoons from 4:00 PM to midnight, and the midnight shirt ran from midnight to 8:00 AM.

Fortunately for me our union contract stated that we must have a minimum of eight hours between shifts if we are called back to work and a person cannot work twice on the same calendar date. That meant that although there were eight hours in between, Ronald could not assign me to work the midnight shift, skip the day shift, and then have me come back for afternoon shift. And believe me he would have done just that if he could have gotten away with it.

154

If I worked the afternoon shift on Monday, I'd have to skip the midnight shift, but would then have to report eight hours later for the day shift on Tuesday. I would then skip the afternoon shift on Tuesday and eight hours later I would report to the midnight shift on Wednesday because it was a new calendar date. Try that for a few weeks and see how your body reacts! I did it for several months. One day I believe I may have bumped into myself coming in, as I was leaving to go out. The only time I got to work the same shift two or more days in a row was when all three lieutenants were working.

As anticipated, I had numerous conflicts with subordinates that I had worked with in the past. In many cases it was a matter of open and blatant insubordination. Everyone in the precinct knew that Inspector Ronald did not like me; therefore they could say what they wanted to say to me without fear of reprisal, especially Sergeant Clarabelle whom I worked for as a patrolman. We did not get along then. In one of our heated exchanges, he commented:

"I didn't like you as a patrolman, I didn't like you as a sergeant, and I certainly don't like you as a lieutenant, which you have no business being."

"Keep running your mouth sergeant and I will write you up."

"You don't have the intelligence to write me up!"

Oh, no he didn't?

Before I wrote him up I went to the commander to discuss the matter. I also complained to the commander about my lack of support from the inspector and others. I told him that my men could say just about anything they wanted to say and knew they could get away with it because of the inspector.

"You are a lieutenant now. Handle it. You don't have to discipline everyone who disagrees with you."

They weren't just disagreeing with me, they were downright insubordinate. After my talk with the commander,

I knew there was nothing else I could say or do. He and the inspector had dug in their heels and nothing was going to change that. I thought when I got to be a lieutenant things would be different. I had more respect and authority than this when I was a patrolman. Lieutenant James Edward Crawford was nothing more than a paper tiger.

However, I didn't just sit around and let them run over me, I don't operate that way. One issue in particular that was offensive to me was when after all of the assignments were made for the shift, and there was one officer still unassigned, if that officer was a black male or black female, the sergeants assigned that officer to walk a one person beat in a high crime area, sometimes on the afternoon shift. If that left over person was a white officer, male or female, the sergeants would take the officer out with them as their driver, or have them work inside. Oh, hell no!

I called in my sergeants and told them there are to be no one person beats on my shift, period. They weren't very happy and one of them said to me in a very sarcastic tone.

"Hey, you're the boss."

I answered just as sarcastically.

"Yes I am."

Although I was no longer running competitively or running with my old cross country teams, I still kept myself in pretty good shape. One of my greatest releases from all of the pressures and stress of the job was running. Many days I would just take off and go, sometimes running eight to ten miles non-stop. It felt great! One of my goals after I started running long distance in high school was to run in the prestigious Boston Marathon. However, because the number of runners had reached five digits, and was still growing, each runner now had to qualify in order to participate in that event. A Boston Marathon runner must have completed two prior marathons with a finishing time of less than three hours and thirty minutes. That left me out. Eventually I worked myself into such good shape that I decided to run in the Detroit Free Press Marathon. I had two goals. The first was to finish. The second was to finish in less than four hours.

I worked my butt off, often running more than fifteen miles per day. Twice I ran twenty miles, and felt pretty good afterwards. I figured that if I could run twenty then I could certainly run twenty six. I was chugging along in the marathon and my time was well under the pace I needed to finish in less than four hours. I was smiling and felt great. Then, it happened. It is something runners read about, but hope never happens to them. At the twenty-one mile mark, I hit the wall. It is the most helpless feeling imaginable. It is like you are driving down the freeway in the fast lane at seventy miles per hour and suddenly your engine cuts off and you can't start it up again.

I could hardly put one foot in front of the other. My muscles were as tight as a drum. After all of the hours I had spent getting ready for this, and after all the miles I had run getting ready, there was no way in hell that I was not going to finish. I literally walked the last five miles, three hundred eighty- five yards. Despite hitting the wall, I came close to reaching my second goal. I finished the race in four hours and nine minutes. I received a medal just for finishing and the city honored and recognized all of their employees who finished the race.

In addition to running, I had a second outlet to release the tension and keep me from going postal. I had made it a point to have at least one positive moment each and every day while on the job. I also promised myself that I would also have a good healthy laugh and that I would help at least one person a day. I didn't always make it, but it wasn't because I didn't try.

1986 Detroit Marathon

One day in particular my laugh came from a woman I tried to give a ticket. As a rule lieutenants do not write traffic tickets. I was one of the few who did. This woman was speeding down the street ten to fifteen miles over the speed limit, in and out of traffic, and tail gaiting behind car after car. In today's terms she would be labeled an aggressive driver. To keep from getting into a long car chase, I got as close to her as possible before turning on my lights and siren. When I pulled up alongside her, she had a scowl on her face and looked like she could eat a nail sandwich. As soon as I got to the driver's door she let me have it.

"What are you stopping me for? Why don't you go after somebody that's doing something wrong?

That is absolutely the worst thing you can say to an officer who stops you, especially when you are in the wrong. I went back to my car to write her a ticket. In fact, I was going to write her three tickets. I reached for my pen, but didn't have one. When I had gotten dressed that morning I forgot to put a pen in my breast pocket. I searched everywhere. I looked in every pocket, the glove box, and between the seats. I even checked the trunk. No pen. I started to ask her for one, but knew I couldn't do that, and there was no way in hell I was going to call one of my officers to bring me one. They would still be laughing today. I made her wait as long as I could before I walked back to her car.

"You're lucky I just got a police run. Slow this car down!"

She snatched her license and registration from my hand.

"You shouldn't have stopped me in the first place."

She then sped off. Of course lieutenants don't get police runs except when an officer requests a supervisor. I had to make up something. I couldn't even write down her license plate number in case I saw her again. That hurt. All I could do was laugh and go buy a pen.

When I got back to the station I was greeted by Inspector Ronald. I did not check to see if he had wet his pants or not.

A complaint against me came across his desk, and as my immediate supervisor, it was his job to investigate it. The incident occurred when I was working the midnight shift. My driver, Darrell, and I, were cruising the lower end of the precinct when we saw some teenagers throwing cherry bombs at passing cars from a restaurant doorway. We stopped and warned them. While we were talking to the "cherry bombers", two men drove up and got out of their car. One had a camera in his hand and aimed it at me.

"Don't take my picture."

He snapped the picture anyway and then took one of Darrell, who also asked that his picture not be taken. Why would anyone be dumb enough to take a picture of a police officer at two thirty in the morning, especially a Detroit cop? They know how paranoid we are. As we approached the men, the man with the camera began to run. I gave chase. As I got closer, the man removed his wallet from his rear pocket and tossed it to the friend who had been standing beside me. Once the friend had the wallet, he began to run in the opposite direction. Darrell chased him. We caught up with both culprits, brought them back to our car, and asked them why they were taking our pictures. They said all they wanted was a picture of a police officer. That answer was unacceptable. If that was all they wanted, then why didn't stop by the precinct during the day? I pulled the film from the camera, exposing it, and then gave him back both the camera and exposed film. We ran a name and warrant check on both subjects and they came back negative.

Three days after the incident Ronald received a formal complaint. In addition to accusing me of destroying his film, the man I chased also alleged that I broke his camera, struck him several times, and used profane language. Darrell was accused of choking the second man into unconsciousness. Darrell was very big and very strong. After the investigation was completed, charges were leveled and a hearing date was

161

set. I chose to have a hearing before the precinct commander rather than appearing before a full police trial board.

I didn't feel there was enough evidence to find me guilty of anything major. I thought that I might get a written reprimand for destroying the film but nothing more. To my surprise, the precinct commander found me guilty of Mistreatment of a Citizen and Excessive Force. I was given a three day suspension without pay. By union contract, I was allowed to appeal his ruling and ask for a full trial board hearing. Darrell chose the trial board only, no commander's hearing.

Because we belonged to different unions, our trial boards were held separately. Mine was first. The attorney representing the police department in my hearing was the same attorney I had worked with on Detail 318, only then he was on my side. He was the one who prosecuted the corrupt officers. He knew about all the threats I had received while on the Detail, knew I was still a little paranoid, and knew that I was still watching my back. It didn't make a bit of difference. He went after me like I had shot someone. He did acknowledge my woes while on the Detail 318 but said they did not justify what I had done to the citizen. I don't think he ever considered the fact that maybe I was telling the truth and the citizen was lying. I was found guilty and my suspension was reduced to two days without pay.

Neither of the complaining witnesses showed up for Darrell's trial board and all charges against him were dropped. Do I think I was set up, of course I do. Following their verdict announcement and sentence, I asked the board if they would include a transfer from Number 13 as part of my punishment. They said they would. After the hearing adjourned I walked over to one of the members on the Trial Board.

"Commander, why did we even bother to have this hearing? Your minds were made up before this thing ever began. This whole thing was a joke."

"Lieutenant, we have to uphold management's decisions."

I literally laughed in his face. When it came to my actual suspension, I was not about to allow my detractors to witness the ultimate embarrassment and humiliation that was about to take place, me turning in my badge and gun. So, I took advantage of a department loophole and petitioned the chief requesting that my two day suspension be deducted from my vacation days in lieu of the physical suspension. He granted my request. However, my name did appear on the next personnel order that lists all suspensions, transfers, retirements, deaths, and was sent to all fifty-four hundred members on the department. It read: Lieutenant James E. Crawford – Two Day Suspension for Mistreatment of a Citizen.

After the hearing I continued to be my gregarious and loquacious self with that big smile on my face and my outgoing personality. They had clipped my wings, but in the style of the legendary Phoenix, I rose from my ashes. Inspector Ronald kept his opening promise to me, and just like in the movie title, I was gone in sixty seconds. My next stop following my suspension was the 15th precinct. I said to myself, "You know, if keep going, I just might make it to all of the city's thirteen precincts before I retire."

Once a Cop – Always a Cop
Paris, France

Chapter Twelve
With Great Authority

The Fifteenth Precinct was the second largest in the city and its problems were proportionate to its size. Racism, alcoholism, and apathy were the standards. It had the largest white citizen population of any precinct in the city, except for possibly Number 16, and it also had the largest number of white police officers and supervisors. Ironically, the top three bosses at the precinct were all black. For the first time in a long time there was no one at the precinct that had a negative predisposition about me being assigned there. Detail 318 had slid into the background, as did my stint on the inspection team. Although I received a large number of grievances, I had more support from my big bosses and some of my sergeants than anywhere I had been so far. Despite all of the grievances I received, the union reps and I often came up with solutions to sticky problems, but it wasn't easy.

Number 15 presented an assortment of challenges, but it was where I shined the most when it came to changing things around, and it was also the precinct where I received the most criticism and had the most confrontations with my fellow lieutenants. I enforced the rules and regulations like I had been doing everywhere else only this time I had the backing of my top bosses. The lieutenants thought the rules I was enforcing were petty and only served to alienate the men.

They really got pissed when they were ordered to do the same with their shifts, something they had not done in the past.

"Crawford is making his men toe the line, so we have to do the same."

They did not have the balls to own up to their required responsibilities and they had to let the officers know that following the rules so closely was not their idea. One of these confrontations became very heated when I submitted a disciplinary report on one of my officers who was routinely abusing his sick time, which was a department violation. For the past several years this officer and others routinely called in sick one week before or one week after his or her vacation giving them three weeks off instead of two. They did this twice a year, year after year. It was brought to my attention by one of my sergeants. Despite being warned, they continued to do it anyway. A fellow lieutenant approached me about my disciplinary write up.

"I see you are sucking up to the bosses again."

"What's that supposed to mean?"

"Didn't you just write up Barker for abuse of sick time?"

"Yeah. So? He was given a chance to stop, but he chose not to."

"That's his sick time. He can use it whenever he wants to use it. You're not a damn doctor. How do you know if he is sick or not? The money is not coming out of your pocket. How long have I been warning you to lighten up and stop poking your nose where it doesn't belong?"

"Right! He just happens to get sick one week before or after his vacation every single year, twice a year? Give me a break!"

"You just don't get it, do you? Your by the book bullshit went out in the '50s. Goddamn! You are in Detroit not the little hick town you came from. We do things different here. When are you going to get with the program and start acting like a real lieutenant?"

166

"Which program is that, John? The one that lets officers come to work drunk, falsify reports, and beat the hell out of prisoners? Is that the program you're talking about?"

As the argument grew louder, officers, other supervisors, and staff workers were tuning in. John pointed to several officers who were looking at us, me in particular, through a glass partition.

"They don't look at me like that."

"I guess not. You kiss their ass, bowl with them, drinks with them, and play softball with them. You're one of the boys! I don't want to be one of the boys!"

John got up in my face.

"In case you haven't noticed, PAL, we're in a war out here. Cops are being shot at and assaulted every day and the only thing you're worried about is if their shoes are shined, reports are neat and accurate and whether or not the prisoners are being read their rights. Fuck their rights! When you stick a gun in someone's face, punch an old lady and then snatch her purse, you don't have any rights. And, if the bastards happen to slip and fall on the way in, and hit their face on the sidewalk, tough shit!"

"Well, PAL, it's because of assholes like you that this department has gone to hell."

"I believe you are the one they call asshole around here."

"Kiss my ass, John!"

"You're a joke, Crawford, a fucking joke."

This Chapter Three of the "Handbook": "Turn Your Head, Close your eyes, and Keep Your Mouth Shut When You See Officers Abusing the System!"

If an officer does not use up all of his or her sick time, he gets paid for it when he retires. However, they don't get the full amount in their sick bank, only a certain percentage. If an officer has built up a large number of sick days in their sick bank, to make sure they use up all of them, they come up with schemes like getting sick before and after a vacation or going on sick leave a month or two before they retire. John was not alone in his opinion. Others also asked me, "Why do you worry about small shit like that, abuse of sick time?"

I didn't think the question was worthy of a response, but it did cause me to review some of the rules and regs I was enforcing. No matter whether I relaxed some of my rules and regs enforcement or not, I knew that there was no way I could ever be like them and stay on this job, but I was paying a dear price for that decision. Was it time for me to take off those rose colored glasses I was wearing and do some bending?

I gave it some serious thought and sought advice from others. They were split in their opinions. Meanwhile I had made it a point to learn the union contracts for both the police officers and the sergeants and to know the police manual from front to back.

I may have set another record, if one were ever kept, for having the most grievances filed against a supervisor. Both unions were very powerful and gave their officers one hundred percent backing even when the grievance was petty. Some of the union negotiations put senior officers, rookie officers and citizens at risk. Senior officers had very little patience with the rookies and did not hide their feelings. I guess they forgot that they were once a rookie.

Unlike most major police departments, back then, Detroit rookies did not work with a training officer for a period of time after graduating from the academy. It was strictly baptism by fire. A rookie left the academy on Friday and started work at a precinct on Monday. On numerous occasions I had as many or more rookies working my shift than senior officers. Many had just graduated from the academy and had never been on the street before, except for in service training or walking a beat. These rookies had no experience dealing with a domestic disturbance, a fleeing felon, or any situations with multiple injuries, victims, and suspects. Add to that the fact they were working a precinct that was totally unfamiliar to them.

Detroit uses mostly two man cars so when rookies were paired together, often they were riding down the street literally looking at a precinct map trying to figure out the location of their radio run. They could have been right around the corner and not known it. Try that at night when you have street signs missing and street lights that don't work. Meanwhile a citizen may be getting his or her ass kicked, a robbery may be in progress, or an officer may need assistance, and the rookie team has no idea how to get there. They certainly wouldn't call for directions over the radio. They would be laughed out of the precinct and if any outside agency or citizen were monitoring that transmission, it would make the six o'clock news.

"Dispatcher, this is scout 10-7. We are new to the precinct and just out of the academy, will you tell us how to get to our radio run. We are at Linwood Avenue and Boston Boulevard right now?"

The logical solution to this problem would be split the officers up and pair each rookie with a senior officer. However, there was one small problem with that; it was against the union contract. All assignments, including patrol car assignments, were by seniority, and a supervisor could not just summarily remove a senior officer from one car and put him on another car if the officer and his partner were both working that day. Senior officers had one refrain, "Pay me extra to train them and I will, but unless you do, they are on their own just like I was when I was a rookie."

I knew I could not split up senior partners, but I did it anyway using the department's mission statement which said that the DPD had an obligation and responsibility to provide citizens with prompt service while at the same time protecting the lives and safety of its officers. I could not have the blind leading the blind, especially when lives were at

169

stake. Of course they filed a grievance against me when I split up the crew, and of course, I lost.

The senior officer also had little or no tolerance for police reserves. Detroit officers were not allowed to work a second job unless they received written permission from the chief of police. Even then, the job could not involve law enforcement or the use of their weapon. The city did not want the liability. This created problems for officers who needed extra cash to make ends meet. The department created a large core of volunteer reservists; each precinct had a dozen or more. They were trained like officers, wore police uniforms, carried guns, and worked alongside the officers. However, they had no arrest powers. The officer had to make the arrest.

The reservists were used mostly for crowd and traffic control at large events. Because the officers could not work a second job, they felt that the city should have offered them overtime to work these events and not use reserves. They saw the reserves as "scabs" and treated them as such.

To make up for this loss of pay, officers came with all types of scenarios to dry up the city's coffers and give themselves thousands of dollars in unnecessary overtime. The detectives at Number 15 and those at the other precincts helped this happen. After all, like John said, it wasn't coming out of their pocket.

Unlike in Florida, in Detroit when a person is arrested on a felony charge, the arraignment process goes through three steps. First, the detectives review the arrest to see if it was legal. If so, they type up a warrant request and the suspect is held in secure detention at the precinct lockup overnight. Second, on the following morning one of the arresting officers takes the warrant request to the prosecutor's office to see if the arrest was in fact legal and if the case is winnable.

If the prosecutor thinks it is winnable it then goes to the presiding judge who makes the final call. If the judge signs the warrant, the prisoner is brought down to court for arraignment and a bond is set. If the judge denies the warrant, the prisoner is released at the precinct. The officer who takes the warrant request to the prosecutor the morning following the arrest automatically receives a minimum of three hours of overtime pay at time-and- a-half whether the prisoner is held for trial or not. This was another union negotiation. The detectives would often send the warrant request downtown knowing it had no chance of getting past the prosecutor much less the presiding judge. Often you would hear the detective say to the officer:

"What the hell, let's give a try. At least you'll get your four point five".

Another ploy to tap the city's coffers was to make an arrest just before the shift ended. These late arrests were often frivolous and the search was often illegal, but it didn't matter. The only thing important was that four-point-five. Recovering a stolen car just before the end of the shift was also a biggie. Often the stolen car was found long before the end of the shift. The officer would disable it and go back later; hoping it would still be there or that some other officer had not spotted it. Most times it was still there.

By the time the officer waited for the tow truck and finished all of his paperwork, he would have his four point five. You'll have to remember that there were a ton of white officers at all ranks that were pissed off about the mayor's Affirmative Action program and they found as many ways as possible to strike back. I had my spies too who were more than willing to keep me up to date as to what was going on in the precinct.

There were black officers who also participated in these shames and collected their four point five. Officers injuring themselves off duty playing softball, basketball, or some other sport, often limped into work unnoticed. They would then trip and fall in front of witnesses. An officer injured on duty is automatically carried as disabled under workmen's

171

comp and the time does not come out of their sick bank as it would if it had not happened on duty. Another union negotiation. The officers saved a lot of their sick days doing this. Coming to work drunk or getting drunk while on duty was another big problem, and it was not limited to just police officers. Every suspension I ever made was due to an officer's intoxication on duty.

I wasn't at Number 15 long when I received a call from a woman who had called for police service. She said the speech of the officer who arrived at her front door was slurred, his eyes were glassy, and she could smell the alcohol on his breath through her screen door. I sent a sergeant out to go meet the officer and bring him to the station. He was just as the woman had described. The sergeant wanted to send him home as sick. As I was filling out the papers for his suspension, I received a tearful call from the officer's wife. She said they were having marital and financial problems and a suspension without pay would be a great financial burden on them. She begged me not to suspend him as did his partner and the union steward.

The most blatant case for me occurred when I was working the midnight shift. A man with a young kid was arrested on felony charges. The kid was sitting on the bench waiting for a relative to pick him up. Suddenly, he disappeared. I went to the back of the precinct to the detective bureau to look for him, and lo and behold, the detective sergeant was sitting with his feet upon his desk, watching television, and drinking a bottle of beer. He had several empties on the floor.

I suspended him on the spot. I notified the field duty officer, who holds the rank of inspector, and he came to the precinct and upheld my suspension. In cases like this the suspended officer appears before the chief the following morning for a chief's hearing. At the hearing the chief determines whether or not to uphold the suspension.

The sergeant apologized, stated that he had never done this before, and asked the chief for forgiveness because he was in his final year before retirement and had never been disciplined. The chief found him not guilty, rescinded my suspension, and returned the sergeant to full duty with no further disciplinary action. The sergeant did not retire at the end of the year.

Needless to say, my stock at Number 15 dropped a few notches. They just didn't give a shit. They were angry for several reasons, especially due to the residency requirement which forced police officers to live in the city. Many of them teamed up and rented an apartment in Detroit, put a few clothes there, and each had a utility turned on in their name. After work they went to their real home in the suburbs. They kept the residency unit very busy.

When I arrived at work each day I did not say to myself, "Okay, let's see what kind of violations I can find today or what can I do to piss off my officers or sergeants." I didn't have to. More often than not, these things just popped up in my face during a routine tour of duty or, as I was going over files, reports, and other paperwork. There were also folks who "pulled my coat" because they too did not like what was going on but did not dare to open their mouths. They knew I would. It was incidents like these that continued to perpetuate my negative image with the officers, sergeants, and lieutenants. In their opinion these were issues that I should have left alone or ignored. I was a trouble maker. I could not have disagreed more. Despite all of these battles, I had made a number of positive changes; integrated the inside staff which was all white when I got there and; integrated some of my patrol cars, in compliance with the contract. The number of grievances filed against me slowly began to drop, and I had back up from my bosses. However, my attraction for trouble or being in the wrong place at the wrong time just wouldn't go away. It happened frequently.

173

On one such occasion, I stopped by to visit a close friend who was a high-ranking officer in the department. She probably shouldn't have let me in. One minute inside, a man walked out of her bathroom. It was my boss. Not my immediate boss, but my big boss, the deputy chief. He was as shocked as I was and looked like the cat who swallowed the canary. I had known him personally for years, and we often disagreed on the way I handled things. He thought I was too aggressive and too impulsive. I did not necessarily agree, but, he was the boss. I cut my visit short. She called me the next day to let me know that he was pissed. Not so much at her for letting me in and catching him, but because I was one up on him. He was married, she wasn't.

On the personal side, I was not the only Crawford sibling living in Detroit. I had two brothers and two sisters who also lived there. With the exception of a brother who lived in Phoenix, and one in Washington D.C., my other five siblings lived in Grand Rapids. My oldest sister, Arvis, lived in Number 10, had seven children, and was probably the wildest of the twelve. She had moved to from Grand Rapids to Philly, and then from Philly to Detroit. I spent one summer with her in Philly. I enjoyed it so much that I actually considered not returning to Grand Rapids for my senior year in high school. I wonder now how that would have affected my life. Arvis was sick frequently, which required her to take a lot of pain medication. I often stopped by to see her.

On my last visit, she wasn't feeling too well. Her speech was a little slurred, she was in a lot of pain, and I thought she was taking more medicine than she should be taking.

Two days after my last visit, I received a call from my mother telling me that Arvis' son had called her and told my mother that Arvis had died from complications of diabetes. She was only forty-six years old, and it was the first death of a sibling. Fortunately it has not happened to me, I've been told that losing a child is worse than losing a parent. My

174

mother took her death especially hard. Arvis' children, who had moved to Detroit with her, eventually moved back to Philadelphia where their father still lived.

When I returned to work after Arvis' funeral, the position of executive lieutenant was about to become available. I was the most experienced lieutenant at Number 15, and the most productive. It was a job I had wanted for years, and is a big stepping-stone toward being promoted to the rank of inspector. Becoming an inspector also would have brought me one step closer to my ultimate goal of becoming a commander, running my own precinct, and wearing spaghetti on the bill of my cap. When the selection was made, a lieutenant who had just been promoted weeks earlier and who had just transferred to the Number 15 received the job. I was hot! There was no way that he was qualified for this position. They also took my pass key to the front office.

I asked the commander why I didn't get the job and he told me that it was not his decision. He said it was the decision of the deputy chief, the same one I had caught coming out of the bathroom. Although I already knew the answer, I had to ask the deputy chief why I didn't get the job. He bounced it back to the commander, saying that he had no part in the decision and that it had been made strictly by the commander. I left it alone. I knew what I was in for from now on at Number 15, especially since they took my front office key. So I conducted a preemptive strike and put in a transfer request to a precinct that was not under this deputy chief's command. To me the handwriting was on the wall and I saw no reason to remain there. This may have been another one of those times when I jumped the gun, or acted impulsively, as the deputy chief had accused me of doing.

I wasn't quite sure if the deputy chief would approve my transfer nor did I know where to go next; there weren't a lot of bosses knocking down my door. However, I did get a message from Melvin, the sergeant I had worked for on

Detail 318. He was now an inspector at the Second Precinct, or Vernor Street Station, as it was called. The network let him know that I had not gotten the exec's job at Number 15 and I was looking for a new home. I don't remember who contacted whom, but he said he heard about the good job I had done at Number 15 and asked me to join him at Number Two. I couldn't believe it. A precinct boss was actually asking me to come and work for him.

It was the start of my eleventh year on the job; I had already been traded more times than Tyronn Leu, and I still had fourteen years to go before retirement. By the way, Tyronn was finally hired as the new head coach of the Cleveland Cavaliers and won the NBA championship. He paid his dues and look where he is now. *Huuuuuuuum!*

I asked myself several times whether or not I should have stayed at Number 15 and just taken my lumps. I knew they were coming. Or, was my decision to leave too hasty? Was it the right one? Were things going to be any better for me at Number 2? And, do I transfer every time I don't like what happens to me? Based on past events, I felt at the time that leaving was the right decision.

Over the weekend, and before I reported to Number two on Monday, I took some time alone to closely analyze my situation and future employment with the Detroit Police Department. I was seriously beginning to wonder whether staying on the job was worth it or not. I was hanging onto a dream that began when I was eight years old, the dream of being a good cop, an honest cop, on an honest police force. Was I living in a fantasy world? Do such departments and do Sergeant Gelderbloms still exist?

The Detroit Police Department wasn't working out. Someone, mainly me, or something, was going to have to change, and soon. My dream began to shatter within months of joining the force and things hadn't gotten any better since. Why was I still trying to hold on to that dream? I guess the answer is that I loved being a cop, making arrests, assisting citizens, writing tickets, helping people, the whole shebang. But, I hated all the bullshit.

The department was corrupt, and not a whole lot of people gave a damn. That's tough to deal with especially when you care so much and not a lot of others do, including the higher ups.

In a *Detroit Free Press* article on May 1, 2006, several former high ranking Detroit officers were quoted as saying the Detroit Police Department was very corrupt. A similar article had been published prior to that on May 6, 1988.

125 DPD officers were under investigation for crack use or crack related robberies. All were hired in the past three years.

Targets are 'street punks with badges'

BY MARGARET TRIMER,
JACK KRESNAK
AND BRIAN FLANIGAN
Free Press Staff Writers

Officers suspected of pulling drug-related street holdups or crack house robberies are the main focus of investigators probing reports of widespread drug involvement among Detroit police, department sources said Thursday.

Reports of officers stealing money and drugs at gunpoint are getting the most attention, one police official said, "because there's always the possibility they might blow somebody away. Suppose somebody recognizes them? They might just pull the trigger."

A police supervisor referred to officers under suspicion as "street punks with badges."

Investigators and police officials,

Angry officers wearing badge of bitterness

The officers interviewed for May 2006 article were officers that I had known personally and had either worked with or worked for during my time on the job. All of them knew what I had gone going through but not one of them lifted a finger to help me. Instead they chose to remain complicit and collect their fats checks and drive their department car. I continued to ponder my situation. I also began to explore the possibility that maybe I was causing much of my own grief.

Maybe I was too rigid and should give in more and turn my head more often. But, that really was not in my DNA. However, when one encounters the same problems everywhere he or she goes, and the animosity against them is so strong and widespread, they have to start taking a close look at themselves as I was doing then. Everyone can't be wrong. What is it about my personality that pisses off so many people? I really am a nice guy, or at least I thought so and so do many of my personal friends and many co-workers. As I thought more and more about my situation, two distinct possibilities came to mind, karma and Murphy's Law. If it is Karma, that means that somewhere along the line I must have pissed off a lot of people and done a lot of mean and hateful things to folks and it was now coming back to haunt me. I really didn't think I did that. I've always believed it was Murphy's Law. However, there is a third possibility that I heard on television describing a cop who was just as dedicated and tenacious as me. They said that he was cursed with the gift for the job. I like that.

Karma: "The force created by a person's actions that inevitably causes good or bad things to happen to that person."

Murphy's Law: "An adage or epigram that says anything that can go wrong will go wrong."

Something was going to have to change. I wasn't sure what it was going to be. I certainly wasn't going back to teaching. These were serious questions that needed to be answered. I enjoyed the rest of my weekend and then slithered across town to my new assignment.

Portland, Oregon Police Department
Once a Cop – Always a Cop

Chapter Thirteen
Same Music - Different Band

Melvin and I sat down and talked soon after I arrived. He then introduced me to Robby, the precinct commander.

"I understand that you know how to run a good shift."

"Yes, sir. I believe I can do that."

"I've got two shifts here that are in bad shape. I hope you can do something with them. If you do, I will make you head of Special Operations." Special Operations is the plainclothes unit at the precinct that handles the major crimes.

"I'll give it my best shot."

"The lieutenants here just let the men do whatever the hell they want to do. It has taken me almost a year to get rid of one of the bastards. I'm working on getting rid of the others. I don't want you coming in here like gangbusters. Just take your time and look the situation over. Melvin and I will give you all the assistance and backing you'll need."

I smiled. I've heard that before. One reason I was able to handle my shifts so well was my organizational skills. I not only used them on the job; I also used them to help ease the tension and pent up frustration that other officers had built up during the day. It was time to bring some innovation to the precinct and the department. So I, with the help of a few others, created a basketball league. Participation was not restricted to just patrolmen. Supervisors were also invited to join. We were hoping the camaraderie created on the basketball court would spill over to the job. It would also give those who thought they still had it, a chance to show off their talent. In addition to the patrolmen, we had two

181

commanders, three inspectors, and a boatload of lieutenants and sergeants join.

On the basketball court there was no rank. There was also no disrespect or hard fouls. The league was an instant success and expanded quickly. Every precinct, bureau, and section was allowed to have a team. We had real referees and a playoff system. The league was named after our chief. We played on Sunday mornings and had a nice crowd each week. At the end of the season we held a banquet and presented trophies. By the end of the second season, I was able to talk the new executive deputy chief into tossing up the first ball at the playoffs.

One of the biggest fans of our police league was the late Earl Lloyd. When Earl was named coach of the Detroit Pistons, he became the first black head coach in the NBA history. At the end of the season when the awards were passed out, I was honored for starting and maintaining the league. Earl presented me with a plaque. I was in basketball heaven.

Earl Lloyd and Me

Meanwhile, at Number 2, I was doing my job and doing it well. The only real conflicts came when I was asked to discipline one officer and let another one go for committing the same violation. I couldn't do that unless there were some really unusual circumstances involved. Each precinct boss had his or her favorites they wanted to protect, and Number 2 was no different. Another thing I had a problem doing was justifying an officer's improper actions in order to prevent the city from being sued and to keep from sending the officer to jail, much like what is going on today with all of the shootings of unarmed black men. I would stretch things as far as I could using department rules and regulations, but there were times when the officer was just flat out wrong and his actions just could not be justified.

One evening a car responded to a house fire. When they arrived the top floor was completely engulfed in flames. A man jumped from the second floor porch. The officers told him to stop. The man kept running. They shot him.

The bullet went through the back of his neck and came out through his Adam's apple. He did not die. The sergeant and the officer firing the shots worked for me so I was given the investigation. Department rules back then required that at least one of following elements be present before an officer can fire his weapon.

- One, to save a life
- Two, to prevent the escape of a dangerous felon
- Three, one of five listed felonies had to have been committed
- Fourth, to save your own life or the life of a fellow officer.

In addition to these guidelines, the officer still could not shoot unless he or she knew with *virtual certainty* that a crime had been committed and that that person had

183

committed the crime. None of these elements were there. They did not know how the fire started; they were not trying to save a life; they had no knowledge that the man was an escaping felon at the time they shot, and they had no evidence that any crime had been committed. All they had was a burning building and a man running from the scene. Maybe the man was just scared or was wanted on a warrant. And, plenty of people just don't like the police and run when they see them.

"Crawford, I need you to justify this shooting."

"Commander, based on what I have now there is no way I can justify them shooting at this man."

"He set the damn house on fire!"

"They did not know that when they shot at him, and it is still not certain that it was arson."

"This is one of my best sergeants. Find a way."

"I've reviewed everything. I can't, sir."

The commander was hot and the assignment was given to another lieutenant who did justify the shooting.

When we covered the topic of "When to Shoot" in the academy, one of our instructors, Sergeant Ronald, was asked a question about the virtual certainty rule.

"If we think a guy has a gun, are we supposed to wait until he turns around and points it at us before we shoot?"

"If there is ever a question in your mind whether or not to shoot, if you are alive to fill out your PCR (Preliminary Complaint Report) then you made the right decision."

I didn't necessarily agree with that statement and Sergeant Ronald really didn't answer the question. If a person does have a weapon that is not visible, it will more than likely be in his waistband, pocket and it will be pointed toward the ground. The officer will most likely have his weapon pointed at the person, his finger will be on the trigger, and he will probably be in a shooting stance. Unless that person is lightning fast, there is no way he will be able to remove that

184

weapon, raise the weapon, aim the weapon, and then fire the weapon with any accuracy before the officer squeezes the trigger. However, we hear it every day, "I thought he had a weapon", and then the execution takes place and the officer is exonerated. This problem will be with us a long time.

On the social side there is one day of the year that most people especially look forward to; the Fourth of July. This is the day for fireworks, barbecue, the family gathers, and lots of fun for everyone. However, this is one day they can skip as far as I am concerned. During my life I have ended up in the hospital on three different occasions on the Fourth of July.

The first time was in the summer of 1955. I had some type of illness that took all of my strength away. I could not walk more than thirty feet without having to sit down and rest. I was huffing and puffing like an old man, and I threw up everything I ate.

My brother Alan had to literally carry me up and down the stairs. My weight dropped down to seventy-eight pounds. I was twelve years old. This had been going on for more than a week, but on July 3rd I felt great. However, the following morning I was too weak to get out of bed again so my mother took me to the hospital. I was diagnosed with everything from mononucleosis, to scarlet fever, to polio. They gave me every test possible, but still no diagnosis. After twelve days of poking and probing, and after I had gained back some of my weight and strength and I stopped puking, they sent me home. There was never an official diagnosis.

July 4th 1981 was much worse. I was at Theresa's house, my girlfriend at that time, when they ran out of Pepsi. How can anybody run out of Pepsi? I went to the nearby convenience store to get a six-pack. As I was leaving the store, I heard brakes squeal and then a thunderous crash. I saw two cars had collided in the middle of the street about a half block away and now steam poured from one of them. I should have taken my ass back to Theresa's, but I didn't. I walked down to get a closer look.

One car was in the middle of the street; the other one was wrapped around a telephone pole on the driver's side. The passenger's door had smashed into the seat after it had been t-boned. The car was leaking gasoline, and an electrical wire from the pole above dangled precariously over the hood of the car. It began to arc. Sparks were flying.

The man behind the wheel seemed to be unconscious. Everyone was just standing around, covering their mouth and, talking to one another, but no one was doing anything to help get the man out. I knew it would just be a matter of time before something bad was going to happen. I went to one of the nearby houses and dialed 911. I told them who I was and asked them to send the fire department and medical help. I found a long ax handle and pulled the live arcing wire away from the car. I asked the people standing around to try to pull the man from the car. They looked at me like I was crazy, and they were right. Within a few seconds that arcing wire popped off the ax handle and hit the side of the car. Sparks and flames flew everywhere as hundreds of volts of electricity passed through the dangling wire and across my body. Standing next to the car in my shorts, I literally caught on fire and was suddenly burnt to a crisp.

My clothes scorched and smoking, leaving me covered with black soot from head to toe. The skin on my arms and legs had fried just that quickly. I was in a complete daze, I began walking down the street. I could hear the people talking about my injuries and saw them pointing at me with fear on their faces as they covered their mouths.

I walked over half a block before someone brought me back to the scene of the crash. The fire department and a patrol car arrived on the scene. The firemen went immediately to the car to free the man after cutting the live wires. I walked over to the officers and identified myself, showing them my lieutenant's badge.

The dispatcher had already notified them that an off duty lieutenant was on the scene. Once they saw my badge, they should have known it was me. As a fellow officer, when you see one of yours, especially a ranking officer, standing there critically burned, your next move is a no brainer. You notify the dispatcher to clear a route to the nearest hospital. They did not do that. Instead, they told me that another car was on the way to transport me to the hospital.

"Officer, I need to get to the hospital, now!"

As they walked away from me they repeated what they had said earlier.

"Sir, there is a car on the way to take you to the hospital. We have to clear this traffic and move these people back."

I couldn't believe what I heard. There I was, a ranking officer with my clothes black with soot, my skin burnt and blistered, and I was arguing with a patrolman about taking me to the hospital.

"I'm about to go into shock. One of you can do traffic and the other one can take me to the hospital."

I was actually pleading with the officer. Most of the people were already back on the sidewalk and the fire trucks had the street blocked. There was no traffic to direct or people to move back. By this time I should have been in the back of the patrol car. The officers' blue and red lights should have been flashing and their siren screaming. That wasn't happening. Beverly, who had worked for me at Number 13 came upon the scene.

"Lieutenant, why aren't you on the way to the hospital?"

"Those son-of-a-bitches won't take me."

"What? I'll take you."

The pain was excruciating. Beverly took me by the arm and began walking me over to her car. I was pretty wobbly. We had walked about thirty feet when the second car showed

187

up. These officers were much nicer and got me to the hospital in record speed, but there was no path cleared to the hospital. The field duty officer arrived on the scene just as I was being put into the patrol car. I was livid!

"Ike, those sons-of-bitches wouldn't take me to the hospital. They just left me on the street."

I had begun to hyperventilate.

"Calm down, Jimmy, take it easy. I'll get to the bottom of this. There will be an investigation, I promise."

That investigation took a left turn before suffering a fatal heart attack on the way to the chief's office. In the end the officers' actions were deemed justified. The ruling was that because I was off duty the officers did not have to obey my order. That was not true. At that time Detroit Police Officers were on duty 24 hours a day, were required to carry their badge and gun, and they were to follow all department procedures as if they were on duty. When I got a copy of the 911 tape of the incident, I could clearly hear folks talking about me in the background,

I spent fifteen days in the burn unit and found out the true meaning of pain. I wore out that morphine drip. The story of my accident was in the paper the next day, pictures and all. I received dozens of cards from well-wishers all around the city. People I didn't know sent me cards wishing me well and a speedy recovery. I even received a card from a man in Jackson State Prison. I also received an ugly card from a cowardice cop. The card was home made. On the front it said get well. Inside it said, "Will all of Lieutenant Crawford's friends please sign below." There were no signatures. I was lying in a hospital bed burned, bandage, and in excruciating pain, and I get this type of card. That is not something you get over in a day or two. And, it was sparked by pure hatred.

Lucky to be alive
Off-duty officer burned in rescue try

By MARTIN F. KOHN
Free Press Staff Writer

There is no such thing as an off-duty cop.

Living proof of this adage — and lucky to be living, at that — is Detroit Police Lt. James Crawford who was badly burned Saturday night when he was shocked by a high-tension electric line while trying to rescue a motorist trapped in a wrecked car.

Crawford, 38, was off duty on the Fourth of July and driving to a store when he saw two cars collide at Harding and E. Vernor. One of the cars slammed into a utility pole. The driver, Charles Holt, 51, was pinned inside. There was spilled gasoline nearby, and a downed power line was "draped over his door," Crawford said.

"All I could think about was pulling him out before the car blew," Crawford said Sunday from his bed at Bon Secours Hospital in Grosse Pointe. Using the wooden handle of an ax provided by a bystander, Crawford moved the wire away from the car while witnesses prepared to lift Holt through a window. However, the wire "curled up and shot back and hit the trunk," Crawford said.

THE ELECTRICAL jolt sent Crawford reeling before Holt could be freed. Holt was rescued by fire fighters and taken to St. John Hospital, where he was reported in critical condition Sunday with multiple injuries in the hospital's intensive care unit.

In retrospect, his rescue attempt probably wasn't such a good idea, said Crawford, who suffered second-degree burns.

See RESCUE, Page 8A

Lt. Crawford; hurt in rescue effort.

7-6-81 — DETROIT NEWS

Rescue goes haywire

Explosion burns cop

An off-duty Detroit police lieutenant is hospitalized with second-and third-degree burns after he tried to pull a live electrical wire from a crashed car Saturday to save a trapped motorist.

Lt. James Crawford is in Grosse Pointe's Bon Secours Hospital with arm and leg burns.

The trapped motorist, Charles Holt Jr., 52, of Detroit, is in critical condition in St. John Hospital. He suffered injuries in the crash.

Crawford said he saw the accident at 6 p.m. Saturday at Harding and East Vernor.

Holt had run a stop sign at the intersection, was hit broadside by another vehicle and pinned against a light pole, said Crawford.

"There were live wires on it (Holt's car) and it looked like it was ready to blow," said Crawford, 38, a 20-year police veteran.

Crawford said people were standing around, trying to figure how to get the trapped man out.

Crawford decided if he could get the wire off the car then they might be able to ease him out a window.

"I took a small ax and pulled it off," he said. "Then all of sudden it flipped back and hit another car I was standing next to."

The electrical explosion knocked Crawford off his feet.

"It burned all the skin completely off my arms," he said. "When I got to my feet I just walked around dazed."

Police pulled Holt from the car and took him to the hospital. The second car struck by the hot wire was unoccupied.

Crawford said doctors told him he would be hospitalized for "at least a week," he said.

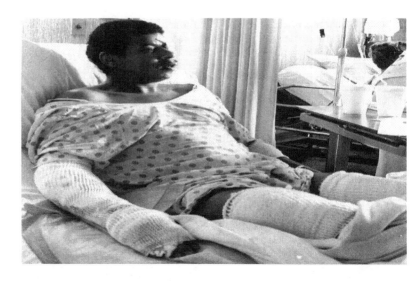

The officer refusing to take me to the hospital was the last straw for Vivian and my good friend George, who was an inspector at the Twelfth Precinct.

"Jimbo, why do you keep putting yourself through this? It's a wonder you're not in a nut house. You may have permanent nerve damage that is job related, take a duty disability and get the hell out of here. You sure as hell have earned it."

"I know George, I probably should."

"Probably my ass! If it were me, I would be in constant pain, I'd be hearing voices, and I'd be walking in circles and talking to myself. Leave, Jimbo! Get your ass out of here. You have nothing left to prove anymore. You are probably the best lieutenant on this whole department and they know that. But they don't support or like you. So why are you staying? Get the hell out."

"I'll think about it."

"Yeah, I know what that means."

190

"We worry about you, Crawfish. We don't want you going off the deep end and hurting somebody. Everyone has their breaking point."

"I'll think it over, Viv, I promise.

And, I appreciate everything you two are saying, but, if I quit now, everything I have done and gone through for these past twelve years will have been in vain. And, believe it or not, there are some officers who do appreciate what I am doing out here. They won't come out publicly, but they have pulled me aside. That still gives me hope."

"You sound like a battered wife."

They both threw their hands up in surrender. And, they were right. I was acting like a battered housewife whose husband kicks her ass, then cries, tells her how much he loves her and that it won't happen again, and turns around and does the same thing a week later. She keeps telling herself, "He really loves me and one day he will change." However, with the Detroit Police Department this is never going to happen, and being accepted by my fellow officers will never happen either. Maybe it was time to get out.

When I returned to work I received a lot of teasing about my electrical burns.

"Hey, lieutenant, my car battery is dead. Would you please touch it so I can get it started?"

"Lieutenant, don't stand too close to the computer. You might erase the hard drive."

I took all of the kidding in stride and even added a few zingers of my own. I earned the nickname "Lieutenant Sparky".

After my release from the hospital, I took some extra time off just to relax, chill out, and to think about the conversations I had with George and Vivian. This proved to be was very therapeutic. I also decided that I could not give up at least, not at this point. I still like police work was still hanging onto that dream. Not only was I a good lieutenant, I

191

also had a sixth sense when it came to spotting crooks and police officers who were going to present the department with problems. The department was full of them, and three of them under my command. Two were in my special operations unit and one was in patrol. Two of them were beginning to get out of hand and the complaints against them were beginning to pile up.

One night I decided to ride with the plainclothes officers. Despite my being there, they were more aggressive than I thought they should have been. One would expect that if your boss were riding with you that you would cool your heels a little. They didn't. I don't know if they thought they were invincible or felt the commander and inspector had their backs. They had even given themselves the nicknames; Starsky and Hutch, the names of two fictitious hotshot plainclothes officers in a popular '70s television series.

"Commander, I think Larry and Walt need to be reined in and work patrol for a while. They are getting out of hand."

My request was denied.

On another occasion as I arrived on the scene of a large disturbance, I saw one of my officers, Richie, kicking a man who was lying face down on the ground. The man was offering no resistance. Three other officers were standing next to Richie as he kicked the man. When they saw me emerge from my car, they scattered like cockroaches. Richie picked the man up from the ground.

"What the hell do you think you are doing? I want statements from all four of you before the end of the shift."

The statements by the four officers brought back memories from eleven years ago when Maurice and I were shot at through the door and the time the officers from TMU shot at the driver of a stolen car. Now, just like those times, the statements of the four officers could have been Xeroxed and signed by each of them. They all said the same thing almost verbatim. No one saw Richie kick the man. It also didn't help that the man was not certain which officer struck and kicked him, but he thought it was Richie. I submitted a misconduct report on the officers to Robbie.

"Let it go, Crawford. This is one you can't win."

"I saw him kick the man, commander."

"And four of the officers said they didn't see a thing. Plus the victim isn't sure who kicked him. How do you win this one?

"Well, will you at least let me take him off the street for awhile?"

"You can't justify removing him from his assignment. The union will be all over you"

I let it go.

The third July 4th disaster came in 1992 when the spine from a catfish went through one side of my finger and nearly came out the other side. The pain was unbearable and I ended up in the emergency room.

It had now been one year since I was critically burned, and I was still feeling some of the effects when I was hit by another bolt, only this time it wasn't electrical. One year prior, Theresa Crawford sat at my bedside trying to pull me through a critical and life threatening injury following my electrical burns. Now, I was at her bedside. Mentally, my mother was a very strong woman. I think that is where the twelve of us got our strength and tenacity. She raised a dozen children, went back to college at age fifty-two got her nursing degree, and worked as a license practical nurse for the next ten years.

However, during the ten plus years after she retired, she had suffered four heart attacks and had by-pass surgery twice. She was now seventy-six years old. Her heart was weak, and she knew it, so did everyone else. In early July she suffered her fifth heart attack. And just as I had done when she had the other attacks, I rushed up to Grand Rapids to be with her. This one was more severe than any of the others, and it made

193

her extremely weak. It scared the hell out of me. In the past she always recovered. In fact, on two occasions she took a trip after getting out of the hospital. This time it was different. For the first time in my life I came to the realization my mother might not survive, and that she may lose in the battle with life. As I stood in her room watching all of the monitoring devices she was hooked up to, I couldn't imagine how life would be without her around.

She was always there for all twelve of us. I was especially close to her and over the years became her right-hand man despite being the tenth child. Because of this close relationship I earned the title of a "mama's boy". I hated it. Many thoughts raced through my mind as I watched her lay helpless in her bed, knowing there was nothing I could do or say to take away the pain she was suffering. There was also nothing I could do to prolong her life. My thoughts drifted back to the death of my father seven years earlier and the recent death of my oldest sister, just two years ago. My mother was dying, and there wasn't a damn thing I could do but watch it happen. She must have felt my presence. She opened her eyes.

"Jimmy, how long have you been here?

I've been here about three hours, listening to you snore."

"Was I snoring?"

"No, I was just kidding. I just got here a few minutes ago."

A minute later, my girlfriend, the other Theresa, walked into the room.

"There's my favorite daughter-in-law to be". How are you doing, sweetheart?"

"Not bad. The question is, how are you doing"

"I'm in a little pain and I've been having some shortness of breath. Other than that, I'm doing okay.

"You hurry and get well so Crawford and I can take you dancing."

She smiled. Theresa and I cut our visit short. I could see that talking was making my mother weak and winded. Just as Theresa and I reached the elevators, an announcement came over the public address system: "code blue, code blue, cardiac care unit, code blue." We rushed back to my mother's room and peered through the glass. She was talking to the nurse. The "code blue" wasn't for her. We stopped by again the next morning before heading back to Detroit. My mother was in good spirits, but also in a lot of pain. The following week I went back to Grand Rapids, this time by myself. I was on my way out of the room when my mother stopped me.

"Are you coming back tonight?"

"Yes."

"I need you to bring my check book, bills and some other personal papers."

"Why are you worrying about bills?" You're recovering from a heart attack and all you can think about is making sure your bills are paid on time. I'm not thinking about those bills."

"Well I am." Please just do what I ask."

One of the things that our parents always preached to us about was paying our bills on time. In the 1950s bill collectors often came to the house to collect their money. I remember several times when my mother hid from the bill collector and I, or my brothers or sisters, went to the door to tell them she was not home. However, when she did have the money, my mother would often go without rather than have a past due bill. I cannot count the number of times that I had chump change in my pocket but did not owe anyone a dime. I still do it to this day, although I am a little better and sometimes make partial payments.

I didn't want to upset my mother, so I reluctantly agreed to bring her bills and checkbook. As I got to the doorway she yelled out, "Bring my insurance policies and a pad of paper."

195

I really didn't want to hear this. I kept walking, never looking back. When I returned that night I brought everything she asked for. She could see by the way I handed it to her that I was uncomfortable with her requests.

"I want you to help me to divide up my things."

"I don't want to hear that."

She just ignored me.

"I have already divided up my furniture. I want you to help me divide up my jewelry and clothing. Some of the kids have already said what they want from the house. I just want it in writing.

"You've already discussed this with them?"

"Yes."

I just shook my head.

"You're not going anywhere."

"Look, I know you don't want to face this, but it's something that has to be done. I've always been able to depend on you in the past, don't let me down."

"Yeah, but -

"Yeah, but nothing. Come over here."

I walked closer to her bed.

"I have lived longer than I thought I ever would. I am seventy-two years old; I have raised twelve children, lived through two wars and a depression. I have experienced the loss of a husband, a child, and I've gone nearly everywhere I have wanted to go. No one lives forever, including me. I have had by-pass surgery twice and have had five heart attacks. I'm not going to keep recovering from these heart attacks. My body is tired. I'm tired. I've watched all of my children grow up and have even seen several of my grandchildren become adults.

Life doesn't owe me a thing. I'm just happy that I've lived to see as much as I have. But, at some point in time your body gives out. It is something that will happen to all of us. I have no regrets. I have lived a full life and I am grateful for that, but no one can live forever."

It is the worst feeling a person could ever have, listening to your mother giving her death bed speech. I wrote down everything she asked, including her funeral arrangements and the songs she wanted sung. It was tough.

When she asked me what I wanted to keep, I almost lost it. I knew my mother was ready to die. I don't know how I held back the tears. It was Fred Hunter all over again. All the police training in the world could not have prepared me for this moment. She had me make out the checks for all of her current monthly bills and told me to pay off the balances with the insurance money that was left over. I said okay, but I knew that was not going to happen. She had paid every bill on time every month since whenever; they got enough from her while she was alive, I'll be damned if they were going to get another penny after she was dead. I visited her the next day before driving back to Detroit.

My mother - Theresa B. Crawford

197

I am not a religious person by any stretch of the imagination. But on two occasions in my life I have had spiritual experiences that defy all explanation. I was told that these are what they call epiphanies. The first one came a week or so after I left my mother's beside. That night I had a dream that she was in the hospital and that my dad was sitting in a chair beside her bed. He was holding her hand as they were talking. As I walked into the room I said to my dad, "What are you doing here. You're dead." Neither one of them acknowledged me. It was as if I were a ghost in the room.

Two days later I got a phone call just after getting home from working the midnight shift. It was my nephew, Barry.

"Uncle Jimmy, this is Barry. My dad just called from the hospital. Grandma had another heart attack."

My heart began pounding as hard as it ever had. I took a deep breath.

"How is she doing?"

"She died."

I couldn't say a word for several seconds.

"Uncle Jimmy, are you still there?"

"Yes, I'm here. Thanks for calling, Barry."

I immediately called the hospital. I had to hear it from them. Surprisingly, they confirmed her death over the telephone. I hung up the phone, sank into a chair, put my head down in my hands and cried like a baby. Ironically, as miserable as I was, that last conversation with her helped me get over the hump. My mother's death was a crushing blow that took a long time to get over. She had prepared me for it as best she could, but there is no preparation for the death of a loved one, especially your mother. For months after her death I cried openly at home, in my patrol car, and occasionally at the station house. I told a friend my dream, and she said that my father had come back to get my mother. I didn't challenge what she said.

Since moving to Detroit I rarely saw my old girlfriend Bette Jo, but we still talked on the phone occasionally. I knew she had gotten a divorce and that her mother had recently passed away. As I was walking out of the church following my mother's family hour, she and her father walked up and offered their sympathies.

We talked a few minutes and agreed to get together at a later time. Soon after, I was making regular visits from Detroit to Byron Center, where her father lived and to Kalamazoo where she lived with her three children. We started dating, and things began to move right along.

One day we were at a track meet for her son. Her daughter Lisa and some friends were sitting behind us. Bette left for a few minutes to get a drink. Lisa was talking loud enough for me to hear her. I don't know if it was intentional or not.

"I think my mother is getting ready to marry this cop from Detroit."

I turned around in record time. My mouth dropped open.

My immediate thoughts were, "Oh hell no!" Marriage was still not in my immediate plans, and I knew that once I retired from the police department that I was going to get the hell out of Michigan and move somewhere where the weather is warm all year around. No more cold or snow for me. I didn't tell Bette about the conversation I had overheard until years later; however, we did have a serious discussion about a possible future together and where we would like to spend that future should we ever decide to spend the rest of our lives together. After all, whatever we had between us had been going on since we were nine and eleven years old, nearly thirty years.

"I've lived in Michigan all my life and I love it here. I like the winters, summers and all four of the seasons, and all of my family is here. I could never leave here."

"Well, I hate the cold, the snow, and the gloomy gray skies from November to June. I'm going to Florida or somewhere. I gotta get away from here."

"Florida is just too hot for me to live there."

We had reached a stalemate. It is like the one a couple reaches just before they get married when one says I want to have children and the other says no way do I want any kids. Compromise is not an option. Whatever feelings we had for each other, spending the rest of our lives together would not be a reality. My visits to Kalamazoo begin to dwindle dramatically, but we did get together whenever I came to Michigan and she stopped to see me when she was in Florida.

After taking some time off, I returned to work at the Second Precinct. However, the atmosphere wasn't quite the same. Ever since I refused to justify that bad shooting, my stock had dropped; despite making drastic improvements on the shifts and in special operations. As it was in other precincts where I was assigned, my troops looked like police officers. My belief is that your appearance is a direct reflection of your self-image. I would be willing to bet that an officer, whose clothes are wrinkled, has food spots and stains on them, and whose police car is junky and dirty, has a house that looks exactly the same. They all go hand in hand.

I was given a couple more investigations where the officer's actions were shaky at best. When I failed to justify their actions, I guess the commander and Melvin figured it was time for me to move on. I was still grieving my mother's death and decided to take some more time off, so I went to the Bahamas for about a week. The night before I reported back to work, I received a call at home telling me that I, along with another lieutenant, had been transferred. I was not given a reason. They said they had been trying to reach me all week. I called the other lieutenant and asked if he knew why we were being transferred. He said he had no idea. It came as a shock to him too. I was to report to the 11th precinct where

I first began as a lieutenant. I had no problems at Number 11 then and hoped that it would be that way again. I took a few more days off.

Maybe I could move here and become chief.
What do you think? (Crawford, Nebraska)

Chapter Fourteen
On the Road Again

S everal days following my involuntary transfer from the Second Precinct, I was still seething and minced no words when asked why I had been transferred, nor did I hide my distain for the commander or Melvin. I stopped by Number 11 to find out what shift I would be working when I reported to work on Monday. My old boss Big John was still there; however, he had been promoted since I left and was now the precinct commander.

"Well, I see you're back."

"Yeah, I just couldn't keep away."

"What happened between you and Robby?"

"I must have worn out my welcome. He didn't want me back when my vacation ended and I have no idea why.

"I don't want you here either."

I smiled. I thought he was joking. He wasn't.

"Don't take it personal."

"How can I not take it personal?"

"You know how petty this department is and how people hold grudges forever? George is still pissed because you went over his head to the commissioner when you worked that bullshit Detail 318."

"Commander, that was over ten years ago!"

"I know. I know. But he hasn't forgotten. He has never liked me, period, or Frank, and he knows we are best friends. He is my new deputy chief and has been giving me the blues

203

ever since I went under his command. And with you here, I know I am going to catch even more hell. I can tell from the look on your face you don't like what I just said, but that's the way it is. Once you step on the wrong toes, your ass will pay forever; you should know that by now. I'm putting you on the dayshift for the rest of the month."

I just stood there. There was nothing I could say.

"Okay. That's it."

There was no handshake; Nothing. He just went back to what he was doing when I walked in.

This conversation with the commander comes from Chapter Four of the "Handbook": "Never Let Them Forget What They Did To You."

As I walked back to my car, two officers who had worked for me when I was there before spoke and offered their hands.

"We heard you were coming back, lieutenant. It's good to see you".

You don't know how much I appreciated that. If you have been paying close attention, by now you should be seeing some patterns being formed. Cops are paranoid, they don't forget, they don't forgive, and they are vindictive.

For the next few months I kept to myself and maintained a very low profile. I didn't rock any boats and made only a few controversial decisions. I let things go that I would never have let go in the past. I was becoming a pussy, and that wasn't me. One of my sergeants and I were going over the duty roster when I noticed that one of my officers had been on the disabled list since the day I got there. He was receiving full pay and benefits and did not have to use any of his sick days.

"What the hell is wrong with Quigley?"

The sergeant looked at me with a smirk on his face.

"What does that mean?"

"He has a bad back. He supposedly hurt himself struggling with a prisoner."

"Supposedly? You don't buy that?"

"The man bowls in two leagues, okay?"

"If you know that, that means that others know it too."

"Yep! Wilson is also disabled. He allegedly hurt his right shoulder when he tripped and fell while chasing a suspect. He also bowls in two leagues as does Lieutenant Bridges."

"Bridges bowls in those same leagues and knows they are both off disabled?"

"Hell, Wilson is on Bridges' shift."

I left that one alone.

After talking to Vivian and George about my conversation with Big John, they became concerned that I was depressed and stopped by to see me.

"I'm tired of being rejected everywhere I go. If I were an asshole, I could see them not wanting me. But, I'm a good lieutenant. I'm a good administrator. There isn't one job on this department that I cannot handle. Not one."

"We know that, buddy, but that's not how the game is played. You know that."

"Well, I'm not going to play any more of their games."

"What's that supposed to mean?"

"My brother has been asking me to come to work for him at this bus company. I'm thinking about it."

"Yeah, right. That will last about ten minutes."

"Excuse me, but aren't you two the ones who said I should leave with a duty disability when I got burned?"

"I've changed my mind. Don't make a hasty decision, okay? Sleep on it. Right now you're upset and aren't thinking straight,"

"I'll think about it and then I'll do it. Okay?"

I managed a smile and left the room.

Before reporting to work that afternoon, I stopped by the personnel office and picked up a retirement packet. I was serious about leaving. George, Vivian and my running buddy, Stanley, who was an Inspector, were the only ones I told I was leaving. I figured that by the time I left personnel, the whole department would know. When I got home I got a call from Stanley.

"Have you quit yet?"

"No, but I'm filling out the papers right now."

"Stop by to see me on your way to work."

As I entered his office, Stanley was on the phone.

"Thank you, sir, I appreciate it very much."

He hung up the phone and looked at me.

"Are you still a quitter?"

"No, I'm not a quitter, I've never been a quitter, but I do know when it's time to get the hell out, and now is that time."

"I'm not going to let you quit."

"Oh, you are not going to let me quit? Who are you now, my father?"

"No, I'm your boss."

"My boss?"

"That's right. Starting Monday you're assigned out to me.

"Excuse me?"

"Don't be late. Now get out of my office, I have work to do."

Somehow Stanley had gotten me transferred to the motorcycle division, simply known as motor. He was an excellent rider and had taught me how to ride a motor scooter and eventually a full size motorcycle. But those big ass Harleys the department uses are a far cry from what I was used to riding. Although I was happy that my friends had gone to bat for me, I still had mixed emotions about staying on the department. But I decided to give it one more shot. During my thirteen years on the department I had not worked at any unit that I could compare to the motor. It was small, elite, and consisted of only thirty police officers. Fifteen of them worked the day shift, 7:00 am to 3:00 pm and fifteen worked afternoons from 3:00 pm to 11:00 pm. Each shift had one lieutenant and two sergeants. I was the relief lieutenant. We didn't work weekends unless we had an escort to do.

Most of the officers and supervisors had been at the unit since its inception. Rules and regulations were more relaxed there than they were at a precinct, and were loosely enforced. The officers were very proud of their unit and went that extra mile to present a spit and polished image to the public. Crisply ironed shirts, neatly pressed pants, highly polished boots, leather bow ties and leather jackets was the dress of the day. Although traffic enforcement was their main function, escorting dignitaries around the city, to and from the airport and providing escorts part of the job description.

My most prestigious escort - Former President
George Herbert Walker Bush

One of the lieutenants at the unit, Bruce, and I had worked together previously and were friends off duty. Our concept of police work and how to get the most productivity from our men wasn't even close. Bruce had been on the job three years longer and had already given into the system.

"Jim, I've been watching you bang your head against the wall for years, and you still haven't learned your lesson. It's like you are watching an instant replay and expecting to see something different from what happened live. It ain't gonna happen, my friend."

"I—I—"

"I nothing. Your problem is that you think everyone is just like you and thinks just like you, especially cops. They are not, and they don't. You are living in a fantasy world and all you are doing is making things harder on yourself and getting frustrated. People on this job do what is easiest, most convenient and best for them to do. They don't care about the system, the rules, the regulations or anything else except themselves. My philosophy is to expect absolutely nothing from these guys and be happy with whatever you get. I sleep a lot better at night."

"You've got to be kidding? You really feel that way?"

"Absolutely!"

Bruce told me up front that he was going to brief his men as to what to expect from me so they wouldn't have any problems when I filled in for him. He said that he told them that I was a stickler for the rules and if they screwed up I will burn their ass.

"The days he fills in for me just do whatever he asks whether you agree or not."

I had worked at Number 10 with one of the officers on Bruce's shift. He told me that Bruce had talk about me coming to motor before I got there. The officers weren't that pleased.

"Why is he here? We don't need another lieutenant?"

"I know why. He's been kicked out of every place else and no one wants him."

"He is also a personal friend of mine and the inspector."

There were a number of incidents that scarred my stay at motor, but only two worthy of mentioning. One occurred

208

when I was filling in for Bruce. As I was reviewing the tickets his men had written and their corresponding activity log sheet, I noticed that the time written on the ticket wasn't even close to the time they had listed on their activity log. What they were doing was writing several tickets during the first two hours of the shift but spreading them out over several hours on their log sheet. Then they would write more tickets in an hour and spread those out too.

What they did during those hours in between writing those tickets, only they and God knows. A ticket that was written at 9:15 a.m. may have been listed on their activity log as being written at 10:00 am, one written at 9:30 am was listed as written at 11:15 a.m. and so on. They had to put the right time on the ticket in case it went to court, but not on their log. Stanley happened to walk in when I made the discovery. Of course now days everything is computerized and tickets are recorded electronically at the time it is written. I was so engrossed in what I was looking at that I didn't realize that he was behind me.

"What the hell?"

"What's the problem?"

"Nothing."

I tried to play it off, but Stanley knew me like a book. He looked at what I had looked at and hit the ceiling. When Bruce came back the next day Stanley lit into him and Bruce lit into me. He never believed that Stanley just happened to be standing behind me when I made the discovery. He thought I snitched. I later found that my men were doing the same thing. I don't know how I missed it.

In the second incident we were on a special detail when I received a call from motor office saying that we were to leave our current detail and report to a church on the Westside for a funeral escort. I was not told whom the escort was for. However, one of the men called the office and learned that the escort was for a drug dealer who had been killed

209

execution style. The request for the escort came from a city council member who was in attendance. We were to escort the funeral out of the city limits and into a new county.

The officers were hot. One officer took it upon himself to notify the *Detroit News*. I gathered the officers and told them to put aside their personal feelings for now and do the escort in the same professional manner as the others. I told them I would handle their outrage. They agreed. The *News* came out and took pictures. I, along with several officers, was interviewed.

"We are an elite unit and we follow orders. We also have risked our lives every day fighting drug dealers. And to have to escort the body of a drug dealer through the city and the suburbs with lights and sirens is not something we are proud of or wanted to do. We had an officer who was killed in the line of duty just last week and we had to stop our escort at the city limits. The men are not happy about this, and neither am I."

OMG! What the hell did I just do?

The chief called a meeting. Stanley was there, our deputy chief was there, and the new executive deputy chief was there. I was the lowest ranking person in the room. The chief went up one side of me and down the other. I immediately went straight to the top of his fecal roster. He said that my comments to the *News* were childish and immature and that I had no right to make them, and that we have a protocol for dealing with the media, and I did not follow it. The new EDC, who ordered the escort, did cover my back, a little, as the chief was lighting into me. He told the chief that he was the one who had given us permission to escort beyond the city limits.

The chief's rebuttal to the media was that the escort was done to facilitate the flow of a large amount of traffic through our city streets and had nothing to do with the person being escorted. He then pulled me aside and said that as long as he was chief of police I would never be promoted again. There goes that promise the mayor made to Frank.

Shortly after the new year began; and due to budget cuts, the department experienced massive layoffs of police officers and demotions in rank. Many plainclothes officers were put back in uniform and were sent to precincts. Some of them had not been in uniform in years. Their uniforms were faded and quite a few did not fit. The uniform store was quite busy that week. Small, specialized units were closed down altogether, including motor. Each officer and supervisor at motor was allowed to pick the precinct he wanted to go to. For the first time in a long time the reason my leaving did not involve drama.

I chose the 14th precinct. My friend Vivian had been promoted to inspector and asked me to come there. Before she extended the offer to me, Vivian talked it over with her boss. She told him that we were good personal friends and that she could use my precinct experience seeing that she had never worked patrol before. She asked her boss what he thought of me.

"I really don't know him that well. But from what I hear he's a damn good lieutenant but everyone likes to use him to do their dirty work, but they don't ever want to back him up. I feel sorry for the guy."

"That's exactly right. That's why I want him here."

"I'd like to put him in special operations, if it's okay with you?"

"You're in charge of patrol. Use him wherever you want to".

Vivian had spent most of her career in the former women's division, recruiting, and working for Frank. Female officers were not allowed to go on patrol in the early years. The only negative side to my transfer, if you want to call it that, was the rumor floating around that Vivian and I were lovers and that she brought her man over to work for her. The word at Number 14 was do not mess with Lieutenant Crawford, he is the inspector's man. The supervisors and officers treated me as if this rumor were true. At least it stopped all the drama and insubordination I had faced at other precincts. Vivian and I laughed our asses off.

I still had the label of being a lieutenant in police officer's clothing. I still liked writing tickets and making arrests. I was now middle management, and lieutenants don't normally make arrests or write tickets. I received a lot of criticism from my fellow lieutenants. By contract, supervisors are allowed to have any driver that they chose. Police officers and sergeants alike knew that when they rode with Lieutenant Crawford they were not just going to ride around and do nothing. They'd be responding to police runs and making arrests. A sergeant I chose to drive me one afternoon asked to be excused.

"With all due respect lieutenant, I've heard about you and how you are out on the street. I am retiring in a month and don't want anything to happen to me before then."

I laughed.

"Sarge, I will take it easy, I promise."

We were on the street less than an hour when we pulled over a car for a traffic violation. The driver was acting very nervous. I asked him to step out of the car. When I looked inside I saw the butt of a gun that he had tried to stuff down in the seat on the passenger's side. The man was alone in the car. We placed him under arrest. The sergeant just looked at me and shook his head. We finished our paperwork and headed back out.

"We are going to respond to just one police run to see how the officers handle it, and then go back to the station. I promise, sergeant."

That one run was a burglary in progress and we happened to be around the corner. We checked the house and found a broken window in the back and footsteps in the fresh snow leading to the garage of the house next door. We shined our flashlights through the window of the garage and saw the stolen loot. When the mother let us in, we saw four pair of wet boots near the front door. I picked each of them up and one boot print matched those in the snow. We arrested the four teenage occupants in the house and recovered all of the loot. We could not turn everything over to the officers who received the original radio run because we had to follow the chain of evidence rules. I kept my word and we did not go back out the rest of the night.

"Lieutenant, I made more arrests tonight than I have made in last five years combined. But I will have to admit, it was a lot of fun. Please don't take me out with you again."

As the layoff ended and officers were brought back to work, motor was reestablished. Anyone who wanted to go back there was allowed to do so. I went back. It only took a few more incidents for me to rekindle my desire to go work for my brother. This time I asked for a leave of absence instead of resigning. The chief had no problem granting my request. He probably hoped I would not come back. I left the department and went to work for my brother.

Once a Cop – Always a Cop

Chapter Fifteen
It Was Time to Go

Although my brother was my new boss, I was still quite nervous the night before I was to report to work. I had worked at the shop several times over the years and everyone there knew me and seemed to like me. Being the boss's brother didn't hurt matters. My new duties included security, both inside and out, and overall maintenance of the premises. For the first time in years no one reported directly to me except a few day workers who were hired to help clean up and dismantle buses. The first month or so I found my new position a bit awkward, and for the first time in the last eleven years I wasn't the boss or barking out orders.

Alan and his administrative assistant, Diana, ran the business that he had started from the ground up over ten years ago. He began on a small lot with two bus stalls and half dozen busses. Now he had several acres, twelve stalls, and was looking to build more. Diana was a little uneasy when I first arrived. I believe she thought I was being groomed to take over and move her out. Alan and I assured her that was not the case. Business was booming and profits were good, however, Alan was not able to come close to the pay I had been making at the police department and my medical benefits were no longer free.

Most of the time I did manual labor and went home at night covered with dirt and grease. It was a far cry from sitting behind a desk wearing a clean white shirt and all that went along with it. The shop was twenty-six miles north of Detroit and going back and forth each day was also taking its toll. I lived five miles from my last assignment in Detroit. Alan had a vacant furnished house on the property and often I stayed the night rather than drive back to Detroit.

I spent a lot of time watching the mechanics. I was trying to pick up some lessons on bus repairs. I learned a few things, but being a mechanic is something that has to come natural. I was struggling. The ground maintenance part I had no problem with. On payday I got to play cop again. Alan paid his employees in cash and I stood by with my .357 Magnum in case someone got the urge to relieve him of some of his money. I was still allowed to carry my gun.

Alan also made his purchases of parts in cash and quite often I found myself traveling to the General Motors parts plant with upwards of twenty thousand dollars in a briefcase. Vendors liked being paid in cash and they offered more incentives for doing so.

I didn't like to stay away from home too long because I had strong feelings about someone being in my house when I wasn't there. I couldn't prove it, but the signs were there. Having lived alone the past ten years I could tell when something was out of place. There were times when I found items had been moved, cigarette smoke still in the air, and once I found a cellophane wrapper on the floor from a pack of cigarettes. I am a non-smoker. What was so odd was that I had a burglar alarm on my house, and it was monitored. It did go off a few times, but entry was never gained and nothing was ever missing. Having worked Detail 318 and for the EDC, I was certain that my telephone was stilled bugged, just as it had been back then. I had a close friend who was a telephone linesman to check it. Bugs were easier to find back then. One day the linesman and I met away from my house.

"If you have anything that you don't want anyone else hear, don't say it over the telephone. Your phone is definitely bugged."

216

A few days after learning my telephone was bugged, I also got confirmation that someone was indeed entering my home when I was away. One Saturday afternoon while working in my yard my neighbor, Oakie, from across the street stopped by to chitchat.

"Hey, Crawford. What's going on?"

"Not much. What's happenin' with you?"

"There's nothing going on here either, things are about the same. I see your alarm went off again the other day."

"What other day?"

"I think it was Tuesday. It didn't ring long. Your cop buddies shut it off."

"What cop buddies? What are you talkin' about?"

"The guys in the burgundy car"

"What guys? What car?"

"There were two guys. Yeah, two black guys."

"You saw two guys at my house?"

"At your house? They were in your house. I've seen one of them there before."

"Why didn't you say something to me?

"I thought you knew. They had a key and went straight in."

"How do you know they were cops?"

"C'mon, Crawford, I'm sixty years old and have lived in Detroit all of my life, you don't think I know an unmarked car when I see one?"

"They had a key?"

"Yes, they had a key"

"No one has a key to my house. No one."

"They sure did. Judy saw 'em too."

"Thanks a lot. I'll have to check into this."

I was baffled. Who in the hell could it be going into my house, and why? I too was convinced that they were cops, and if so, that meant they were probably following me and knew when I left for work, got to work, and left to come home. I asked Oakie to keep watch and to call me next time he saw them go in. Their cover must have been blown because there were no more visits from my brothers in blue.

While Alan ran his own bus company, he was also the deputy director of transportation for the city of Detroit. Like me and my other eleven siblings, Alan was also quite feisty and spoke his mind, even when he shouldn't have. Alan was an appointee of the mayor and, as such, marched to the mayor's beat. One day Alan decided to march to his own beat and the mayor didn't like it. The rift between them escalated, got very ugly, and made the newspaper and television headlines for several days. When the dust settled, Alan was fired and the city attorney charged him with fraud involving the contracts he had signed with the city for bus repairs. Because he was a small businessman and his cash was limited, he often received advanced funds which were deducted from his bill to the city. The charge was that he and the bookkeeper for the city conspired and padded the advance payments. The bookkeeper supposedly received a small fee.

The special unit that had been investigating Alan allowed me to bring him down to police headquarters to turn him in. I tried to get him released into my custody, but they would not hear of it. The mayor wanted him behind bars. As the arresting officers came out of the courtroom to take Alan into custody, my jaw dropped. I couldn't believe what I was seeing. One of the arresting officers was Edgar.

"You have got to be shitting me?"

He could not look me in the face. He had just been at my house a month earlier when I called him to change my locks and alarm code after Oakie told me that officers were in my house. Edgar was the one who had installed the original alarm and he was a locksmith. Final confirmation of Edgar's involvement came after I got home from surrendering Alan to Edgar. I asked Oakie to describe the black officers he saw entering my house.

"He was at your house a couple of weeks ago. You know, the guy in the brown pick-up truck."

That was Edgar. I had been asking for help from the fox who was guarding the hen house. The City of Detroit, Alan's biggest client, cancelled all of his contracts after the arrest and his business took a nosedive. With the loss of business and five figure legal fees, he could no longer afford to keep me on the payroll. Meanwhile, my bills were piling up and I had tapped nearly all of my savings to make ends meet. I had two choices, find another job or go back to the department. I chose to go back and return to motor.

Once a Cop – Always a Cop
Hinsdale, New Hampshire

Chapter Sixteen
The End of the Road

After turning in my reinstatement papers at personnel and going over to motor, I was stopped by Commander Jessie. Motor and his unit were housed in the same building. Ironically he headed up the unit that investigated and arrested Alan, and as I would learn later from his secretary, I was also being investigated. I had only met Commander Jessie two or three times, and all we ever did was to exchange greetings. This time he pulled me aside.

"Crawford, I hear you are coming back and I'm glad to see that. From what I hear you are a damn good lieutenant. But you have to learn when to pull back. You can't keep bumping heads with everyone, especially the big bosses; that is, if you plan on getting ahead in this department. I'm not asking you to be a wimp, just choose your battles a little better than you have in the past. We all have our principles, but sometimes we need to compromise and take one for the team. You are not a team player and everyone knows that, and that is why you keep getting bounced from precinct to precinct. If you cannot turn your head sometimes and not see what you saw, or on occasion do something completely against your principles, you will retire as a lieutenant. Do you understand what I am saying to you?"

"Yes, sir, I do."

"There are only two ways you get promoted around here. Actually there is also a third way but we're not going to talk about that one. You have to know someone that has the ear of the mayor or the chief and they have to say to the mayor or chief that James Crawford is a great lieutenant and should be promoted to inspector. Despite some of the good things I have heard about you, you don't have that. And if you continue down your old path you never will. Your future is in your hands and the hands of your sponsor, and right now you don't have a sponsor. You need one to get promoted".

Thank you, commander. I'll do what I can."

"Good luck, lieutenant."

Damn! You never know who is watching you. But, everyone seems to know me and has an opinion of me. Am I the topic of conversations off duty or at executive meetings? And, how do you just abandoned thirty five years of upbringing and life lessons just to get a promotion? With the mayor pissed off at Alan, and the chief telling me that as long as he is chief, I won't be promoted, I'm not sure a sponsor would be of any help. However, I still had close to 10 more years to go before retirement. Maybe the chief and the mayor will both be gone by then.

A few days before I was scheduled to return to motor, the department had promotions and Stanley was promoted from inspector to commander. .

"Why in the hell didn't you tell me you were being promoted? I would have been there.

"I figured you would find out eventually."

"Where are they sending you?"

"Number 10."

"If you think you're going to leave me down there at the Motor unprotected, you're crazy. You don't know a damn thing about patrol, so you'll need a good executive lieutenant. Guess who that is going to be?"

222

"Excuse me ex-lieutenant, who is not officially back on the job yet. How are you going to tell me who to make my exec?"

"I just did, commander!"

"I don't even know the procedure for getting an executive lieutenant.

"All you have to do is get me transferred to Number 10 and name me your exec, it is that easy."

Of course I had no idea how the procedure worked, but I was going to find out. I knew I would be getting the job. I was finally taking that next step toward being a precinct commander. Maybe I'll get that spaghetti after all.

Stanley was even more of a stickler for the rules and regulations then me and he was a spit and polish man all the way. Number 10 was about to get a double dose it might not be able to handle. When the network sent out the word that Stanley and I were both coming to Number 10, transfer requests started flying.

When we got there, the building was in terrible shape. The area around the front desk was dirty, and the floors looked like they had not been mopped or waxed in weeks. The walls were in dire need of paint, and the parking lot was cluttered with trash. The outside of the building also needed painting. Administratively, it was just as bad. Reports that were long overdue were still sitting in the wire baskets of the patrol inspector, Patricia, and those reports that were alleged to be complete were sitting in the commander's basket, full of errors.

A check of the logbooks revealed that many of the monthly reports had not been submitted in nearly a year. How the third floor had allowed this to go on so long is baffling. I guess that when the inspection team went on hiatus the precincts went back to their old habits. When Stanley saw all of the delinquent and erroneous reports, he hit the ceiling. He and Patricia had it out the first week. The two of them had a

223

history, and apparently it was not a good one. She had already drawn battle lines before we got there. She didn't like me anymore than she liked Stanley. However, she out ranked me, so I had to follow her orders, even though I reported directly to Stanley. My reporting directly to Stanley did not go over very well with her either. For that reason and many others she wanted a transfer and made no secret about it.

Patricia became very disruptive and kept a lot of drama going. She made it clear that she and Stanley could not co-exist at the same precinct. I took the advice of Commander Jessie and kept a low profile through all of this. It didn't take long for Patricia to get her wish. She was transferred to the 15th Precinct.

Her replacement was Clyde. Clyde and I had known each other for years and got along very well. In fact, he was the field duty officer on duty when I suspended the detective sergeant at Number 15 for drinking on the job. Clyde had thirty-four plus years on the job and was just bidding his time until his retirement in a few months. We had a sit down the first day he was there.

"Crawford, I haven't worked in patrol in so damn long it's a shame. I'm going to have to depend on you a lot until I get the hang of things. I know that both you and Stanley are hard workers and do everything by the book. I'll try to do the same, but it's going to take me a while for me to catch on, so you'll have to be patient."

I would have to be patient? This was coming from an inspector. I was just a lieutenant. I loved it.

"The first thing I'm going to do is to take that vacation I had scheduled before I got transferred. I imagine you will be the acting inspector while I'm gone."

My face lit up like a Christmas tree. Acting inspector, I liked the sound of that. Clyde hung around a few more days before starting his vacation. Stanley began a clean-up project right away, starting with the filthy floor in the lobby. The grass around the precinct was also groomed. The building was painted inside and out, and he stayed on the officers about their appearance. When I came on the job 15 years earlier supervisors enforced the dress code more strictly, especially the wearing of the hat.

Back then the hat had to be worn anytime an officer was outside the precinct station, which included wearing it inside the patrol car. That requirement was lifted during my rookie year. Finally, someone other than just me was enforcing the rules. I used a little humor to get some of the officers to comply. We had an officer who may not have shined his shoes since joining the force. One day I took some money from my pocket and with a smile on my face I walked over to him.

"Officer, do you need to borrow some money to buy some shoe polish?"

He looked down.

"I'll take care of it, sir." He didn't think it was funny.

Officer Williams had an Afro and his hat literally would not fit his head. He often left his hat in his locker. He had no intention of wearing it.

"Officer Williams, is your barber on vacation?"

"No, sir"

"Did he die?"

"Lou, my hat messes up my Fro."

"I have a pair of scissors on my desk if you need them. You need to start wearing your hat."

The next day he walked into my office with his hair stuffed under his hat.

"Doesn't this look stupid?"

"I think it looks great."

I had all I could do to keep from laughing. It looked absolutely horrible.

"Yeah, right!"

225

I didn't press the issue anymore after what I saw and I wasn't about to tell him to cut his hair. It was a part of his personality. I do make exceptions sometimes. From that point on we just joked about it. Sometimes he would walk into the station holding his hat in his hand. When he saw me he would raise it up in the air to let me know that he had it with him. I would then give him the thumbs up.

We had a female clerk that was on permanent light duty and wore civilian clothes. One day as I passed her at the front desk I had to do a double take. I called her aside.

"Greta, that is a very lovely bra you are wearing, but I shouldn't be able to see it."

Greta was wearing a sheer see through blouse.

"Do you have another blouse or a jacket in your locker?"

"Yes, sir. I'll change it."

Of course I could not have said that today without being charged with sexual harassment and I am certain that this was not the first time she came to work was dressed like that.

As the executive lieutenant, all correspondence coming into the precinct went through me. One of my first jobs was to go through the mound of mail each day and screen it for both Clyde and Stanley. I also had to review all reports sent to Stanley, requests to the chief and requests from police officers, sergeants and lieutenants. I wrote responses to the chief and others on Stanley's behalf. I was in charge of timekeeping, Neighborhood Watch, school safety officers, community relations, and I approved the leave days for the sergeants and police officers.

Being in charge of Neighborhood Watch and Community Relations, I was required to attend neighborhood meetings. I listened to the complaints from citizens and instructed my officers and sergeants to do whatever they could to resolve them. I made myself available to anyone who wanted to talk, and I loved it. Being in charge of the scooter patrol at the schools gave me an opportunity to visit them. I wanted to see

226

how much things had changed since I left Northern. They hadn't.

I had a great support staff of both my officers and sergeants. A dream that had begun to shatter over a decade ago now seemed a real possibility. It looked as though I was finally going to become the officer I had always wanted to be. I had the job I wanted and a boss that backed me up. But then there was the chief who said I would never be promoted under his watch. I'd have to work on that.

All requests to Stanley had to go through me first. Everyone at the precinct was aware of the close relationship between him and me, so quite often they made their 'pitch' to me before they made it to Stanley. I pretty much knew what he would approve or would not approve. Because I had so much precinct experience and Clyde and Stanley did not, and because I was the most visible and vocal, it was widely thought that I was actually running the precinct. Nothing could have been further from the truth. Stanley and I locked horns repeatedly, and I usually came out on the losing end.

However, unpopular decisions he made and I passed on were often attributed to me, and there was absolutely nothing I could do about it.

Things quieted down after Patricia left. When Clyde returned from vacation, I went back to being the exec. My duties kept me in the office almost the entire day and that's how Stanley wanted it. He knew I was a magnet when it came to finding the bad guys, and he did not want me leaving the station unless I was going home. He didn't even want me going out to lunch because he knew I would get involved in something I shouldn't have. My days of writing tickets and making arrests had come to a screeching halt. Not only did I make a lot of arrests on duty, I made a lot off duty. Shit just seemed to happen around me.

Off duty I could be walking toward the store and a guy would run past me with a woman's purse in his hand that he had snatched. I'd be in a parking lot and see guys trying to break into a car. There was a convenience store around the corner from my house that had a huge parking lot. Young, thuggish looking guys would park in front of my house, four doors away from the store, and then walk back to the store. A few minutes later I'd see them running to the car, jump in, and speed off. So, when I saw them pull up and walk to the store, I would call for a car and the officers would be waiting for them down the street.

On duty, it was the same way. As I pulled alongside stopped vehicles, I could see that the driver was nervous as hell. In the subsequent investigation, I would find some contraband or a weapon, the person was wanted on a warrant, or the car was stolen. It happened over and over again. The few times I did sneak out or was on precinct business, I ended up making an arrest or taking some other type of police action. Stanley would just shake his head.

The peace and calm at Number 10 was short lived. When Stanley ordered the sergeants, through me, to clear up that backlog of overdue reports, and gave them only a month to do so, my stock dropped rapidly. Just keeping up with all of the daily paperwork was hard enough for them. Redoing the old reports pushed them to the brink, and they thought it was totally unnecessary. As the sergeants and lieutenants reviewed the past due reports, they bitched and complained to me nearly every day.

"These reports are six and seven months past due. What's the point in submitting them now? The information is old."

The only response I could give them was, "Because that's what the commander wants." Personally, I agreed. Most of the information in the reports was outdated and useless. We should have started over from the day Stanley and I came in.

I tried to maintain my policy of having that one good laugh every day and doing something positive to help someone. One day as I was returning from a Neighborhood

Watch meeting I saw a woman, who looked to be in her late seventies, shoveling the snow in front of her house. We had gotten three or four inches earlier in the day. I was in full uniform, gold bars and all.

"Why are you out here shoveling this snow?"

"I need to clear a path to my door. You know the mailman won't deliver if he can't get up the steps and to the box."

"Don't you have anyone who can do this?"

"My grandson usually does, but you know young people these days. They come when they get ready."

"Good bye—go---go—go."

I shooed her away and into the house. I not only cleared a path to her mailbox, I shoveled the entire sidewalk. She came out when I finished.

"How much do I owe you, officer?"

"Thirty-five thousand dollars." She laughed.

"I don't have that kind of money."

"Call me when you get it."

"Alright." "Thank you, officer."

I had done my good deed for the day. I was hoping that none of the neighbors thought that this is what police officers do. And, I hoped none of them called the station asking for an officer to come out and shovel their sidewalk.

Over the next nine months I had my share of battles with the shift officers and shift sergeants. Things were slowly slipping back into that "here we go again" mode. The most painful incident was the death of Officer Williams. I was on vacation at the time and saw on the news that he had been shot to death while responding to a radio run. I immediately called the station. One of the lieutenants, whose nickname was "Smooth" answered the phone. When I asked what happened, he said Officer Williams and his partner were walking up the steps on their run when the owner opened fire on them.

"Was Williams working plainclothes?

"No, he and his partner were in uniform. The owner said he thought they were burglars."

"If he was in full uniform, and it was broad daylight, how in the hell could the owner mistake him for a burglar?"

"I don't know. He must have panicked."

When I returned to work I noticed that there was an air of hostility from those who had been friendly to me before my vacation. It persisted for the next couple of days. I finally had to ask one of my staff members what was going on. She pulled me aside.

"Who did you talk to about Williams' death?"

"Stanley."

"Anybody else?"

"Smooth answered the phone when I first called, and we talked about it."

"The story is that the first question you asked was "Was he wearing his hat? That is why they are pissed. Supposedly you said that if he had been wearing his hat he might not have been killed."

"You're kidding, right? You are kidding me?"

"No, I'm not JC. I tried to clear it up, but they wouldn't listen. They were just looking for something to be pissed about."

"Who started this lie? Smooth?"

She just looked at me, rolled her eyes in disgust and walked away.

Smooth was perhaps the most well-liked lieutenant at the precinct. He was easy going, kept a smile on his face, laughed and joked with officers constantly and I don't believe he ever wrote a disciplinary report since becoming a supervisor. He was the patrol officer's ideal boss. I made a few inquiries as to how the rumor got started but was stonewalled at every point. No one wanted to say who started it. It eventually faded away.

To help cope with and maintain my sanity, I did what relaxed me the most, running. I had never really stopped. The times when I was totally flustered and frustrated, I would put on my running shoes and take off and run for miles. I also went to the University of Detroit and played racquetball and basketball. On one of these trips I met up with a young, teenage looking student who was the star of U of D's girls' basketball team. Her name was Renee. She was twenty-one but could have passed for eighteen. I was forty-one, but looked to be in my mid-thirties. She began to flirt. I just laughed. I knew she had no idea how old I was. She kept it up, so I flirted back. Before I left we exchanged telephone numbers. I knew from the beginning that this was not going anywhere, but I was going to enjoy the chase.

Back at the station, unpopular decisions made by Stanley were still being attributed to me. One of these decisions was to remove two plainclothes officers from their assignment. The officers had been getting more and more complaints about their overly aggressive behavior on the street. Stanley had had enough. He ordered me to put them back in uniform. When this same situation came up at Number 2 and I asked that Larry and Walt be put back in uniform, my request was denied. Stanley was of a different mindset, and I was glad. When the officers learned of their pending transfer back to uniform, they hit the ceiling.

They spent the evening getting tanked up and made their way to my house. I would not let them in. They let loose a barrage of profane threats and told me they would be waiting for me when I came outside. They were drunk as skunks. I don't know to this day why these officers, Sergeant Clarabelle and others felt they could talk to me or threaten me in this manner and get away with it. I had a reputation of being a tough, no nonsense lieutenant. Maybe my frequent smile and outgoing personality gave the appearance of me being all bark and no bite. Based on what had happened to

231

me in the past, I had no reason not to believe the two officers threat. I notified Stanley and he notified Internal Affairs. Stanley, the field duty officer, and I met at the station. A lieutenant from Internal Affairs arrived a short time later. The lieutenant from I.A. was ordered to go by the officers' houses and take them into custody. The officers were nowhere to be found.

The following morning we learned that one of the officers had gone to the psych ward at Detroit General Hospital stating he was suffering from extreme mental stress caused by Lieutenant Crawford. He was not the first officer to do that. This was a common ploy used not only against me, but also used against other supervisors by officers citywide. When officers felt certain they were about to be suspended or arrested, they would commit themselves and say they were under duress. They would then use this defense at their disciplinary hearing. On several occasions I was named as the culprit causing their mental stress. Dozens of officers received duty disabilities using this technique.

For the first time in more than ten years, I began carrying a backup gun strapped to my leg. Until the officers were physically located, I also kept a loaded shotgun in my office. This was no way to live. A rumor quickly circulated that I had been seen sitting in my office wearing a bulletproof vest and had a loaded shotgun propped up against my desk. The rumor went on to say that the officers at Number 10 feared for their lives because they thought I was going to flip out at any time. This prompted several calls from close friends who were worried about me.

I assured them the story was not true. I had had about all I could take, and my ulcer was beginning to flare up again. The medical section refused to declare my ulcer as duty related forcing me to use my sick time instead of disability time. The pain was too much for me to come to work. The only thing keeping me going at that time was Renee. We had begun seeing each other and she was full of spunk and was just what the doctor ordered. Of course I took a lot of teasing. Some of the comments were downright nasty.

"Crawford, is that your daughter?"

One of my brothers ridiculed her to her face and told me that I should be ashamed of myself. When I told Tracey about Renee, she said she would not speak to her. While the other, older women I was dealing with had their hand stuck out and were pushing hard for marriage, Renee was trying to make life for me as comfortable as she could and it wasn't costing me a dime. We played basketball; she took long runs with me, and we played touch football and softball in the street. She gave me full body massages like the ones her team trainer gave her and the rest of the girls. We played cards and board games. Strip poker was our favorite. Of course when you lose you have to take off an article of clothing. I think we were both losing on purpose. After three or four hands we said the hell with this and hopped into the sack. We shook the hell out of those sheets those nights and nearly every day of the week, sometimes twice a day. They say men hit their sexual peak around the age of forty. They were right on.

I eventually met all of her family. Renee's presence in my life caused me to do several things I vowed that I would never do. The first thing was to allow her to move in with me. The question now was how we were going to explain to her mother, who was three years, my junior, why Renee was moving out of her dorm and into my house? I had met her mother several times at basketball games and she seemed to like me, but I am sure that in the back of her mind she was wondering,

"Other than the obvious, what the hell does this old fart want with my child?"

Her mother and I joked about what we should call each other. She wanted to know if she had to call me Mr. Crawford since I was older than her. I asked if I had to call her Mrs. B. We settled for Jimmy and Helen. I attended all of Renee's home games and some road games. She had no problem introducing me to her teammates.

Any doubts that Helen may have had about me were pushed aside when I healed a wound that had been eating a hole in her heart the last several years. Helen had remarried and she and her second husband had a young child, Marcus. That marriage also ended in divorce. Helen got custody and the ex received liberal visitation rights. During one of these visits he decided to keep Marcus permanently and did not return him after the visit.

Helen did everything she could to locate the two including hiring private detectives. The ex kept in contact with Helen by sending pictures of Marcus as he was growing up and Marcus kept in contact with his mother with the letters he wrote her. The letters were mailed to Helen by the ex-husband's mother who steadfastly denied that she knew the whereabouts of her son and grandson. It had been more than five years since Helen had last seen Marcus.

I contacted a friend who worked for the Department of Justice and he was able to locate both the ex-husband and Marcus. They were living in California. I had Helen update the custody order and then we took the trip west. We had local law enforcement meet us at Marcus's school. Helen presented the principal the paperwork and I flashed my badge to make the trip seem official.

The principal brought Marcus to the office, but Helen was asked not to say a word.

"Do you know who this woman is?"

"Yes."

"Who is she?"

"She's my mother."

With tears rolling down her cheeks, Helen nearly squeezed the life out of him. We asked them not to notify the ex until we got on the plane. Helen did not prosecute him for kidnapping, but the threat to do so and implicate his mother kept him from ever trying to take Marcus again.

After returning to the station I had become a virtual mummy. I didn't give a damn about anything. Everyone could see that I wasn't the same Lieutenant Crawford that had come there 15 months ago. In addition to the things that were happening to me on the job, I was beginning to become more frustrated with the caliber of officers the department was hiring. A lot of them looked and acted like thugs with their gangster hats, flashy jewelry and their lingo. Had I still been working the street, there were several I would have patted down for drugs or a weapon. One afternoon two young men who looked like they had just left the dope house passed me in the hall and started down the steps toward the officers' locker room.

"Excuse me. Where are you two going?"

"To the locker room, sir."

"And why are you two going to the locker room?"

"To get dressed."

I had a puzzled look on my face and by now they realized that I did not know they were police officers. They flashed their badges.

"Damn!"

We had female officers who were drawing big salaries from the department while still on welfare. They were also getting food stamps and other benefits. When they got caught, they were allowed to plead guilty to a misdemeanor, pay back the money, and stay on the job. I couldn't believe it. We also had an active officer who was shot to death trying to rob a dope house. The most interesting scenario was when a sergeant recognized an officer that he had arrested several years ago for stealing a car. This officer had pleaded the charge down to a misdemeanor and then had the arrest expunged from his record. Police agencies still have access to

235

expunged records for all job applicants. He never should have been hired. Somehow he slipped through the cracks.

Another officer at Number 10 was arrested for trying to sell his gun to buy crack. This was not what I expected when I gave up my teaching career. For something that started out so positive when I came to Number 10, and raised my hopes of getting those oak leaves, my optimism took a nose dive like no other. I wasn't sure how much longer I was going to be around. I was clearly at the end of my rope. At this point you may be asking yourself, "Were there any supervisors on the DPD who gave a damn and followed the rules and regs like you did? The answer is "yes". Question number two would logically be, "Then why aren't they going through the same flak that you are?"

I would never dare to compare myself with President Obama. He is way above my persona and intellectual level, and I have the utmost respect and admiration for him. However, there are similarities. As a couple and as parents, he and Michelle, with their girls, are perhaps the most well-liked family in America. He is smart, friendly, very likable and has a constant smile on his face. Despite what the Republicans would want you to believe, most people, regardless of their race, would love to have him as their next door neighbor.

As far as that first part is concerned, I put myself in that same category. My friends, co-workers, and even many of my subordinates like me as a person, but just as it is with the President, they don't like my policies and some of the decisions I make. However, in his case, once the media, or in my case, once my fellow officers, put you on the radar screen in a negative light, and then build on that negativity with every new decision you make that they don't like, even if what you are doing is the right thing and in their best interest, they still take you to task and make you the villain. The Republican Party has tried to crucify him because of the

Affordable Care Act, better known as Obamacare. The new Congress has already introduced legislation to repeal it. It is his Achilles heel and they have not let up. The electronic media, newspapers, social media and others have kept the negative drive going and continued to do so his entire presidency.

Nearly anything controversial that he proposes comes under close scrutiny and criticism, and his detractors descend upon it like a bunch of locusts, especially during an election year. He has been labeled by some as the worst President ever because of all of this negative reporting even after bringing the country back from the brink of total disaster. He cannot get a break. I feel much that same way. No matter what decision I made, it was the wrong one and pissed somebody off. As it turns out, the ACA has helped tens of millions of people to become insured when they could not be insured before its passage. Despite its success, every Republican candidate in the 2016 presidential campaign vowed to repeal it if elected. Despite the good he has done, he has been the most disrespected President in the nation's history.

I needed a break, and Renee gave me that break. Over the next eight months things were going great between Renee and me. I couldn't wait to get home after a hard and frustrating day at the precinct. However, I noticed that she seemed to be having a lot of colds lately. She was sniffing and sneezing all of the time, was not eating, and was losing weight. I talked it over with Helen. She told me that she suspected that Renee might be using drugs. Renee had told me up front that sometimes she smoked weed, but nothing stronger. I told her that if she was going to stay with me, that was a no-no. Things began to get worse. She finally admitted to using crack. How could I have not known this? I had been dealing with drug addicts for nearly seventeen years.

I had no idea what to do next. She was the best thing that had happened to me in years, but I couldn't have her bringing dope into my house and I could not date a woman addicted to drugs. A few months after Renee and I began seeing each other, Tracey had finally come around. Actually she and Renee became very close. Maybe it was because they were only a few years apart in age and thought alike. Tracey also suspected that Renee was using drugs, but never told me nor did she know that it had gotten so bad.

"Daddy, I know how you feel about drugs. I really like Renee. Please don't put her out. See if you can get her some help."

I was both pissed and happy. Pissed that Tracey had not told me about Renee's drug problem, but happy that she was concerned enough to go to bat for her. Renee agreed to get help. I took her to a drug rehabilitation center.

If someone had told me that one day I, a lieutenant on the Detroit Police Department who had never even smoked a joint at age forty-two, would be taking my live in girlfriend to a drug rehab center for treatment, I would have called them crazy. Yet, there I was. As we toured the center, it reminded me of the place in Coldwater, Michigan where my parents had taken my sister, Joan. Joan was a year and a half older than me and was the most quiet of the twelve, the most likable, and never caused anyone any problems, but she did not have a happy life. As with all families, especially large ones, there is always going to be one child or two who needs more love, affection, and attention than the others.

In our family it was Joan, but she did not get it from our parents or the rest of us. I am not sure if any of us knew how to give and show love toward one another like other families did. We were dysfunctional back then and still are today. But that is a whole new book to be written. Joan was smart, but like me, she also did not like school. However, instead of just getting by with a passing grade like I did, she chose to skip classes, spending most of the day in the lavatory and therefore received failing grades.

Because of this, her trifling ass counselor made an immediate and erroneous diagnosis and labeled Joan as a slow learner. My parents were left with three choices. Joan could attend that special school in Coldwater; she could be placed in the room known as the "Dumb Room" at Central High with slow students who spent the entire day repairing shoes, or they could stay in her ass and make her attend classes. They chose to send her to Coldwater.

The place was absolutely horrible. The residents walked around like people from the television show, *The Walking Dead*. They slobbered and gurgled all day, had glassy eyes and they stunk. The place smelled worse than a nursing home. Every time we left, Joan cried and said she did not belong there. I agreed, but, I was only thirteen and there was absolutely nothing I could do about it. I felt terrible. After nearly a year, my parents finally realized it was a mistake and brought her back home.

By then the damage had been done. Her stay there had a devastating effect on her life all the way into adulthood, until she met and married Larry. From that day on she was as happy as I had ever seen her. They were absolutely crazy about each other, and she finally got the love, affection, and attention she had been seeking since early childhood. The five children they had may be the proof of that love and affection, or maybe it they just wanted a lot of kids. Whatever it was, it was working.

At age forty-seven, Larry died of a heart attack. Shortly after his funeral, Joan became very ill. We thought it was just part of the grieving process. However, when she went to the doctor a few days later she was diagnosed with fourth stage ovarian cancer. Ten weeks later Joan rejoined Larry. Joan was forty-six. Like Joan, Renee was in tears and said she was not like the people we were looking at, and that she did not belong there. This time I did have a say so. I couldn't leave her at that place.

She promised to get help and Helen agreed to take her somewhere else. That never happened. Renee's addiction was worse than any of us thought and she would not accept my help or help from her mother. Helen and I both knew that she would probably have to hit rock bottom before we could get her the help she needed. I finally had to ask her to leave. A short time later I received a call from Helen telling me that she thought Renee was living in a suspected dope house and she was worried sick. The house was in Number 10 and she wanted to know if there was anything I could do. I was off on leave at the time. I got two of my sergeants who I had been personal friends with for years and who I fully trusted, to go by the house and get her.

They knew what they were getting into, took the necessary precautions, and had a back-up team nearby. I kept my fingers crossed and hoped that nothing would go wrong, like a physical or an armed confrontation. There was no lie I could tell that would be big enough to cover what I had asked the sergeants to do for me. They put their lives and careers on the line for me and it was greatly appreciated. There were still some who were on my side and had my back.

They brought Renee back to Number 10 where I waited for them in the parking lot. When she got into my car, she looked absolutely terrible. Her clothes were dirty, her face was dirty, her hair was all over the place, and she smelled to high heaven. Renee's personal hygiene and having an exceptionally clean house had always been one of her most important concerns. She seldom had a hair out of place. She often showered twice a day, and smelled great. Often when I got home I could smell the Pine Sol as soon as I opened the door and more often than not, dinner was on the table. She couldn't stand a dirty house and changed clothes more often than any other woman I had ever dated. This was her doing; I never asked her to do any of this.

I looked at her with pain on my face.

"What the hell happened, Renee?"

"I don't know."

"Just look at you."

"Just take me back, okay?"

"Back to a dope house?"

"That's where I want to be. Please take me back."

I sat and stared at her for a while. She couldn't look me in the face.

"Your mother is worried about you, and so am I."

"I'll call her."

"No you won't. You know that, and so do I"

After a few more minutes of listening to excuses, I knew that there was absolutely nothing else I could say or do for her. She was going to be like this until she decided she had enough. I had the sergeants drop her back at the house and I called Helen to let her know what happened.

In addition to dealing with the garbage at Number 10 and my attempt to rehabilitate Renee, Alan's second trial was coming to a conclusion. The first trial ended in a hung jury for him and a not guilty for his alleged co-conspirator. I will never understand how they were able to charge him with conspiracy the second time. You cannot conspire with yourself.

In the second trial the judge did not allow Alan to use the defense he had used in the first trial, but he and his attorney were not made aware of this until the trial actually began and he wasn't given time to prepare a new defense strategy. His conviction was a slam dunk. Alan had never been arrested in his life and his conviction was for a white collar crime. In most cases like this, first time offenders are usually given probation, have to pay restitution, and are given a hefty fine. Alan was sentenced to six months in prison. In Detroit, most

six month sentences are served in the county jail, and the
defendant usually gets two months off for good behavior.

When Alan left his business one morning headed to court
for an evidentiary hearing, he never returned. The judge said
that Alan was late for court, revoked his bond, and sent him
across the street to the Wayne County Jail. Five hours later
Alan was on the bus to Jackson State Penitentiary. Alan had
embarrassed, humiliated and pissed off the most powerful
man in Detroit political history. He had to pay for that. He
served the entire six months. As hard as Diana tried to
prevent it, his business went down the tubes. He eventually
ended up losing the business he started from the ground up.

That six month sentence took a toll on him both
physically and mentally. He was never the same after that.
Much later in his life Alan had two triple by-pass heart
surgeries with lingering effects. Alan and I were born on the
same date thirteen years apart, and often celebrated our
birthday together. Alan was now living in a nursing home
just outside Detroit. He was in a very poor health. Our
birthday was coming up soon and I did not think we would be
celebrating many more together. I gathered as many family
members as I could and we held a birthday party for the two
of us at the nursing home. Less than two months later Alan
died. He was eighty-five years old.

After my encounter with Renee and my returned to work, I
sat at my desk meditating and going over the boatload of
scenarios that I had experienced over the past seventeen plus
years in both my personal and professional life, and I did not
like what I was recalling.

However, there was one common chord resonating
through nearly every conflict and confrontation I had had up
to this point; over ninety per cent of the officers and
supervisors I had these conflicts with were white. Every
officer I had suspended over the years was white, and all
were suspended for the same reason, being intoxicated while

on duty. Add to that another common chord; nearly all of the precincts and units I had worked at were predominantly white, that is, until now. Number 10 did not fit that mode. It was predominantly black in every aspect, and nearly all of the conflicts I was having now were with black supervisors and black officers. That certainly rang a bell in my head and started a whole new thought process on my part.

Although the confrontations with the white officers and supervisors were more frequent, more vicious, and more personal than those with the black officers and supervisors, nevertheless, these conflicts and confrontations with the black officers were still taking place. This could lead a logical thinking person to reach the conclusion that maybe the problem wasn't the color or rank of the officer I was having conflicts with. Maybe the problem was me.

I was just beginning my eighteenth year on the job; I had eight more to go before retirement. I was at the best place I had been in years, had support from my friends and boss, had the job I had always wanted, had he office I wanted, yet here I was, still engulfed in conflict with supervisors and officers just like all of the other assignments.

I was at a major crossroad and had to ask myself, "Do you really want to go through eight more years of this? I sat there several more minutes, quiet and focused, when my self-analysis session was interrupted by a knock on my door. It was one of my new rookie officers.

"I'm sorry to bother you sir, but do you have an extra ticket book holder? I've been writing a lot of tickets, but it's kind of hard when you don't have anything to write on. They ran out of them at the uniform store."

"No, Polly, I don't. I'm sorry."

"That's alright, sir. Thank you anyway."

As she began to walk out of the door, I called her back.

"Wait a minute."

I reached into my drawer and pulled out my metal ticket book holder. It was a fancy one with all types of compartments and a sturdy writing surface. It was a rather expensive one. Since Stanley had grounded me, I really had no use for it anymore.

"You can use this one until you get one from the uniform store."

"Thank you, sir, I will be sure to put it to good use."

She began to walk out of the room for the second time when I called her back again.

"Polly, keep it. It's a gift from me." Suddenly, a huge smile spread across my face. Just that quickly I knew that the moment had arrived. It was a great feeling, a feeling that a person has when he or she finally decides to end a bad relationship that they had been hanging onto for years, a relationship that was abusive, mentally draining, and wasn't ever going to go anywhere. It was a relationship that your family and friends had been telling for years that you needed to end. But it wasn't their decision to make. It was yours. You were the one who had to say to yourself, "I deserve better than this". I had just reached that point. It was time for me to leave.

Today was going to be my last day of work as a lieutenant on the Detroit Police Department.

I finished my day shift and later that evening, I called in sick for the following day. I told them my ulcers were acting up again. Shortly after the midnight shift had gone out on patrol I went back to the precinct with a car full of empty boxes. I parked my car near the back of the precinct where my office was located and walked around the front and through the lobby. I had to pass the front desk to get to my office.

"Hello, lieutenant," said the desk sergeant. "I thought you were off sick?"

"I am. I forgot that I had a very important report due in the chief's office in the morning. I just came in to finish it up."

He looked at me like I was crazy. That was the quickest lie that I could come up with. I walked to the back, unlocked the back door, and brought my boxes in.

I kept the blinds shut in my office. As I was sneaking into my office with more boxes, a plainclothes officer walked up.

"Lieutenant, what the hell are you doing here this time of night?"

"I have a report that's due on the chief's desk in the morning. I just came in here to finish it."

The officer, who was a lot older than me and had close to thirty years on the job, looked at the boxes I was carrying and then looked at me.

"Bullshit. You're packing it in, aren't you?"

"No. I told you what I was doing here."

"Lieutenant, you are leaving. I've seen that look before and you have a ton of empty boxes."

"I'm not going to argue with you. I told you why I was here."

"I've never had the opportunity to work directly for you, but I believe I would have enjoyed it. I think you are a damn good boss. I might not get anyone else to agree with me, but I believe it. Whatever you do or wherever you go, I wish you the best of luck, sir."

"Thank you very much. It's nice to know that someone around here likes me."

"Let me clear out before you tell anyone, okay?"

"You got it."

We shook hands and then I entered my office with the boxes. I stopped in the middle of the floor and looked around at the pictures, awards, and other plaques on the wall. I looked at my stereo system, the television, the leather swivel chair and all the clipboards I had hanging on hooks with vital information. In the corner were the police scanners that I listened to throughout the day. This was how I had always pictured it before I joined. This was the type of office I had always wanted. This was the job I wanted, only at a higher rank. But hell, this was close enough. There would be no spaghetti on my hat.

As I removed each picture, award and plaque from the wall, I savored the pleasant memory or imminent danger involved. As I removed papers from my desk drawers, mementos and pictures of my children from the top of my desk, it was difficult. When I see professional athletes standing at a podium announcing their retirement and choking up, tears rolling down their cheeks, I now know what they are going through. Leaving something you love is tougher than you think.

Despite all of the problems, everything in this room had played a major role in my life for the last seventeen plus years. After loading up the car, I came back in for one final check. I sat at my desk one more time and leaned back in my chair. As I scanned the bare walls and the empty room, I realized that my feelings and my life were both as empty as the room, especially now that Renee was gone. I was going to have to find a way to start over. I got up, laid my door keys on the desk, turned off the lights and pulled the door closed. After walking a few feet, I realized I had forgotten something. I went back and removed my nameplate from the front of the door. It read, Lieutenant James Crawford.

My only decision now was what method I was going to use to leave the department. I could resign, take an early retirement, or request a duty related disability. It didn't take long to make up my mind. Now I had to prepare for the battle ahead.

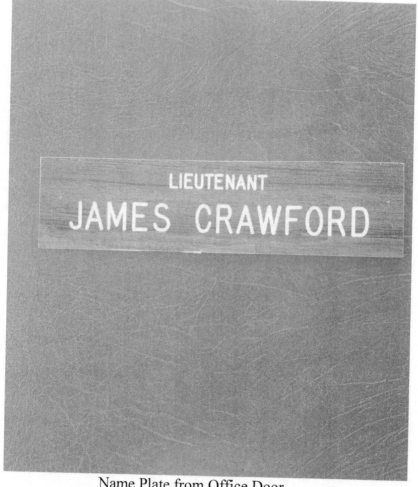

Name Plate from Office Door

Once a Cop – Always a Cop

Chapter Seventeen
The final Battle

I took a much-needed rest the first week after my unofficial retirement. I had not informed anyone except George and Vivian as to my future plans, not even Stanley. The following week I went to the medical section and advised them of my plans to seek a duty related disability due to job related stress. They told me my chances were slim to none, but I was welcome to try.

Although the medical section greatly influences whether or not an officer will get a duty disability, they don't make the final decision. That decision is made by an eight-member panel which has sole control over who gets a disability and who does not. Two of the board members are from the two police unions; two are from the firemen's union, and four are mayoral appointees. One of the mayor appointees is the chief of police or his designee, an executive officer.

An officer requesting a duty disability for stress is required to see three psychiatrists. One hired by the police department, one of the officer's choosing, and one hired by the pension board. The burden of proof lies with the person requesting the disability. However, even if all three doctors state that the stress or injury was not duty related, the board can still grant the disability. It is very subjective. The psychiatric reports are only used as a guide. The benefits and salary of an officer receiving a duty related disability greatly outnumber the benefits and salary of those who receive a non-duty disability. The difference in pay and benefits is tens of thousands of dollars more over the years. I had already seen three department psychiatrists due to my ulcer, so I already knew what they thought of me. I now had to find a good one of my own, and, I did.

History had taught me to document everything in writing that was the least bit controversial, to keep copies of reports, and to keep good copious notes on any major meeting or event and as you can see from the news articles and pictures. I did just that going back some forty plus years. These documents, plus my old diary, and other notes I had taken were extremely helpful in preparing my case and for recalling some of the personal conversation I had with others. The disability process takes several weeks. Fortunately, I had accumulated enough sick days, personal days, court time, and vacation days over the years to keep me on the payroll until the decision was made. However, had they chosen to play games with the time clock, I would have been up the creek without a paddle.

In preparing for my battle before the pension board, I was strongly advised to get a good lawyer and to get the names of the individual members on the Board and do some politicking. That wasn't my cup of tea, but sometimes you gotta do what you gotta do. The battle was exhausting, both mentally and physically.

Many times I had to stop to take an afternoon nap, and often after I found myself crawling into bed at night. I was asleep as soon as my head hit the pillow. All the lawyers I tried to hire wanted at least a five thousand dollar retainer. I didn't have it. I received a copy of the psychiatric report from my doctor and the department's doctor. Both psychiatrists agreed that I was stressed out and should no longer remain a member of the Detroit Police Department. However, the department psychiatrist went on to say what he had to say to keep the department from paying me and to keep his checks coming in. Oddly enough, I think both of their reports accurately summarized in a couple of pages what I have been trying to point out throughout this entire book. My shattered dream may not have had anything to do with me joining the Detroit Police Department. This is the heart of what the department psychiatrist wrote about me:

"I think he is qualified to be a police officer and strikes me as a decent, honest type person. He is likable, quite intelligent and is rather serious minded. I don't think he would benefit from any type of psychiatric care and I don't think he would accept any. I think that because of his personality peculiarities, he has a tendency to be overly repressed. I feel that Lieutenant Crawford's stress is a result of his upbringing, childhood experiences, and his father's drinking and death. The death of Lieutenant Crawford's mother, his strong sense of right and wrong, and his strict enforcement of Department Rules and Regulation were also major contributors to his stress. My conclusion is that no matter what job he would have held, or whomever he worked for, he would have been just as stressed out due to the factors mentioned above. Therefore, the Detroit Police Department is not responsible for his stress and a duty disability should not be granted."

Damn, he's good! But, looking at other jobs I have held, he was absolutely right. I thought about my resistance to passing the failing students at Kettering just to keep the failure rate low. I thought about the problems I had later when I was the emergency management coordinator at a Bethune where important and vital reports could be turned in days late and no one seemed to give a damn but me. Then there was my stint with the Department of Juvenile Justice whose policies allowed a four-foot-eight, ninety pound nine year old who threw a rock through a window, and was subsequently charged with Throwing a Deadly Missile into an Occupied Dwelling, to be handcuffed, shackled, and shipped to court alongside a six foot one, two hundred pound seventeen-year old who was caught selling dope on a street corner or breaking into a house.

Both crimes were classified as a twelve point felony, and all twelve point felons were held in secure detention overnight and sent to court the following morning. Sometimes the kid was so skinny that the handcuffs did not fit and kept slipping off his wrists. Imagine the affect this had on them. He was being a kid and was doing what kids his age do, throw rocks. His rock just went astray and landed in someone's living room.

I could see the fear in their eyes and on their face as the tears rolled down their cheeks. I often used a technicality to reduce their point total to eleven and then sent the child home with their parents. I was chastised by my boss for doing this. She said I was abusing the technicality and ordered me to stop. I did. However, I could no longer participate in this farce, so I left. To me becoming part of the problem simply because it was easier than being part of the solution wasn't the answer. There were several jobs I wanted to try after I retired, but, I promised myself that if any of them became too stressful, I would leave. Detroit had used up all of my stress.

My psychiatrist disagreed with department psychiatrist and offered this assessment:

"The Detroit Police Department wrote rules and regulations they knew were unenforceable. Any supervisor who followed these rules as written would have suffered the same fate as Lieutenant Crawford. Further, the lack of support from higher ups on the department, the multiple death threats, the cutting of his brake line, the removal of his lug nuts, and his assignment to two controversial details caused his stress. He was set up to fail and he did. Therefore, it is my conclusion that the Detroit Police Department is responsible for Lieutenant Crawford's stress, and he should be granted a duty disability."

The second conclusion reached was as compelling as the first, and I also agree with it. So here we are with two strong arguments as to why I am where I am and what caused it. It was now a tie. I never received the report from the pension board psychiatrist. Could it be that my greatest assets, my honesty, integrity, and strong sense of right and wrong were also my greatest liabilities? If this is the case, how does someone like me survive in a world or atmosphere where these assets are the exception rather than the rule? Is this why so many people hate their jobs and hate going to work but are afraid to speak out in fear of losing that job, and end up with ulcers, hypertension, and other debilitating illnesses?

After receiving the department's psychological report, I was allowed to respond. I wrote an extensive report listing dates, times, incidents, the whole nine yards. I attached copies of written reports verifying my accusations. The department then responded to the report by my psychiatrist. They totally disagreed with his diagnosis. Now, all I could do was to wait for the hearing.

A short time later it all came to a head. I received a call telling me that my hearing was set for the end of the following week. I asked the clerk how much time I would have to present my case to the board.

"You won't be appearing before the pension board."

"What are you talking about?"

"It really isn't necessary and very few ever do it. The board's decision will be based on psychiatric reports and the written arguments and rebuttals submitted by you and the police department."

"You mean to tell me that my whole future depends on whether or not my rebuttal is stronger or better than the department's?"

"I'm afraid so, sir. I'm sorry, that's the way it is." I was as frustrated as I could be. I called George and Vivian, but either one was in. George did return my call a short time later.

"I see that you called. You sounded like you were upset. Is everything okay?"

I told George about my conversation with the secretary the pension board.

"Is that what you're worried about?"

"Yes. Do you know someone that's on the Board?"

"How about the chairman?

"The chairman?"

"Yes, the chairman is my boss, Commander Ryan."

"Can you set up a meeting for me with him?"

"Of course. When do you want it?"

"Yesterday."

"He just walked in. I'll talk to him and call you back."

George called back and told me that my meeting with Commander Ryan was set up for the next afternoon. I met with Commander Ryan and gave him copies of the report submitted by the two psychiatrists and a copy of my rebuttal. We discussed the reports for over an hour.

"The firemen and policemen usually scratch each other's back and vote for each other. That will give you four votes, that's all you'll need. We'll need a fifth person there to have a quorum, which will be me. We seldom have more than five members in attendance. I really don't think you have anything to worry about."

I had an ally on the board now and all I could do was to sit back and wait for next Thursday's vote. It was only Wednesday. I wasn't sure if I was going to last that long. I stayed as busy as I could trying not to think about it. However, doing that was like listening to Sweet Georgia Brown and not thinking about the Harlem Globetrotters.

The day of the hearing I got a call from Stanley. He asked me to come to the station to go over some reports that I had turned in before I left and to discuss a complaint that had been filed against me by the medical section. One of the doctors and I had gotten into a loud and heated argument concerning the cause of my ulcer and I called him a quack in front of a room full of people. At that point I knew I would be gone soon and really didn't give a shit about anything I said or did. As far as I was concerned, the entire Detroit Police Department could go to hell, including the doctors.

"Have you heard anything about my hearing?"

"We'll talk about it when you get here."

My drive to Number 10 was probably the slowest it had been in seventeen years. All of my thoughts along the way were negative. I began to question Stanley as soon as I walked into his office.

"What happened at the pension board hearing?"

"We'll get to that. Let's go over these reports first."

I can't remember to this day what was in any of those reports and I really didn't care. And, I could care even less about the complaint from the medical section. I was going to be leaving the department no matter what. Stanley and I finished our paperwork.

"Well, what's the verdict?"

"The vote was three to two. Both police unions voted against giving you a duty related disability."

"Surprise, surprise."

"Both firefighter unions and Major Ryan voted to give you the duty disability. Congratulations!

Stanley offered his hand. I left with a big "giddy up" in my step. I'm not sure if my feet every hit ground between Stanley's office and the parking lot. As I opened my car door and put one foot inside, I looked up at the precinct building, flipped the bird, got in and drove off.

I asked George what was Commander Ryan's favorite drink and he said vodka. I stopped by the liquor store and bought enough liquor to last him until the end of the year. I thanked both he and George for their help.

As I was making my final preparations to leave, George stopped and paid me a visit.

"Well Jimbo, what's your next move?"

"George, I am getting the hell out of Dodge."

"Where are you moving to, Southfield?"

"Southfield? I'm leaving Michigan."

"Where are you thinking about going?"

"Somewhere where it is warm all year around. I am sick of this ice, snow and these cold ass temperatures. My first two choices are Arizona and Florida."

"Damn, you don't play do you?"

My hearing was in November. I put my house up for sale, packed up all of my belongings, said all my good-byes and never looked back. Six months later I was in my apartment in sunny Florida.

I wrote about my tenure on the Detroit Police Department in my 1992 novel titled, *Officer in Trouble: The Detroit Cop who Refused to Play The Games.*

After writing *Officer in Trouble,* I went back to Henry School where my dream began and presented then retired Lieutenant Robert Gelderblom an autographed copy of my book. The local media covered my visit. He was elated. He did a few magic tricks for the students just as he did when I was there forty years earlier and received a huge ovation.

Lieutenant Robert Gelderblom who started it all

The Grand Rapids Press

THURSDAY, SEPTEMBER 24, 1992

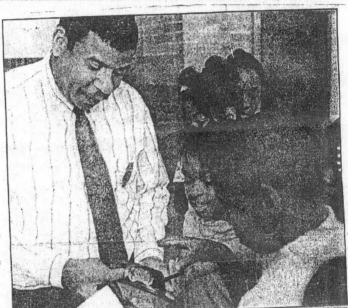

PRESS PHOTO/JEFFREY BROWN

Nyesha Northern and Maricello Riley, foreground, look at badge of former Detroit officer and writer James Crawford.

SUCCESS STORY

Former Henry School student credits police officer role model

By Lawrence R. Heibel
The Grand Rapids Press

In 1955, as an elementary student at Henry School, Grand Rapids native James Edward Crawford dreamed of being a police officer like Robert Gelderblom, the public safety officer who visited his school.

Wednesday, Crawford, 49, of Orlando, Fla., returned to Henry School to give Gelderblom the first copy of his self-published novel – based on his career as an officer.

"This is where it all started. I wanted to let him know that after all these years he got through to one person and made a difference in my life," Crawford said.

Crawford presented the book to Gelderblom and spoke to a group of fourth-, fifth- and sixth-graders, trying to impress on them the importance of having the courage to do the right thing.

"Listen to your parents. Listen to your teachers. A friend who tried to get you to do something you shouldn't be doing isn't your friend," Crawford told them.

Gelderblom entertained the children with a few magic tricks, just as he did when he spoke to Crawford's class nearly 40 years ago.

"Find someone you can trust. Listen to him and don't go astray," Crawford told the students.

Crawford was in Grand Rapids to distribute his novel "Officer in Trouble – The Detroit Cop Who Refused to Play the Games." He said the book is a thinly disguised autobiography chronicling his trials as a police officer who tried to follow

see SUCCESS, D4

257

Closing Thoughts

Being a police officer is one of the most difficult occupations in the entire world. People think they know what is like to be a cop and what we go through, but they really don't have a clue. No matter how hard you try to visualize it and try to put yourself in our shoes, unless you have worn the uniform you will never, ever, know what it is like. In addition to making split-second, life and death decisions, the pressure on rookie police officers to comply with and not go against their fellow officer is enormous, spelled with a capital "E" and it never lets up. There are only two words in the English language that come close to describing the pressure placed upon a rookie officer. Those two words are *pure intimidation*. As an officer, if you do decide not to take that tainted path and go against the clique, you will pay dearly for that decision.

Contrary to popular belief, except for the officers who are bullies and are looking for a confrontation, some police officers are often just as afraid of the people they are investigating as are the people being investigated. Many of these officers have had little or absolutely no contact with people of color until they came on the job. The only thing they know about us is what they see on television or read in media reports. Many of these virgin officers have never had a black friend, gone to school with a black person, had a next door neighbor who was black, or had a black person teach their children. And they know absolutely nothing about black culture or history except the stereotypical stories that say most black people have no initiative, embrace welfare and food stamps, and have absolutely no desire to find or keep a job.

The picture they have etched in their mind is based on what they see daily on the nightly news. What they see are

258

black men with dreadlocks and a large amounts of facial hair being placed in the back of patrol cars, black men with guns stuck up in someone face, and black people carrying protest signs because we are angry at what we have been experiencing over the years at the hands of police officers and those officials who support and justify their actions. And they are seeing black folks burning down business establishments. So when they join the police force and are assigned to patrol a predominantly black area, based on what they have read and seen, and based on what they have been told by their friends, they are already in a defensive mode and are expecting and preparing for the worst.

With that state of mind, the least bit of provocation will accelerate them from the defensive mode to the attack mode, which often results in a fatal encounter and the obligatory cover up that follows. This is talked about in a *New York Times article*, "When Police Don't Live in the City They Serve" by John Eligon and Kay Nolan.

Just as city and police officials point out that the corrupt officers we are seeing in the videos only represent a small fraction of the police force, equally, we as a black community point out that the litany of images showing black men being arrested and committing these egregious acts only represents a small fraction of our community, but somehow our message never gets through.

Reporting the acts of both groups, the street criminals and the criminal cops, grab headlines. They glue audiences to their televisions and are good for the ratings; therefore, they receive the most and constant coverage.

For the bigoted and corrupt officers, who like leopards, will never change their spots, there are remedies. Only by removing their sense of entitlement and exceptionalism through more criminal prosecutions, only with unions curtailing their backing of criminal acts by these officers, and only with the erosion of the undying support by their fellow officers, will it stop them from doing what they have always done and always gotten away with. Accomplishing this goal is a long way off.

However, the picture is not totally bleak. There is hope for the young officer; education, training, and real community policing will close the gap and be a giant step toward removing fear on both sides of the fence, and can very well result in a positive relationship with the people in the area they are assigned to patrol. I hope both scenarios happen, but to be very honest and realistic, I do not expect to see either one happen during my lifetime.

Epilogue

During the first five years following my departure, the Detroit Police Department fell apart. I mean it went from sugar to that other stuff in a hurry. I recently had breakfast in Detroit with about twenty retirees, and they said the department has hit rock bottom and they are embarrassed when they see the caliber of officers working the streets. When I joined the department we had 5400 officers, were running six to ten cars per shift at each precinct, and were still barely able to answer police runs in a timely manner.

They say that number of officers on the street is now down to 1500, the starting pay for rookie officers is $14.95 per hour, and precincts are now only running two or three cars per shift. Service is atrocious. They said you'd get a quicker response by calling the state police. My research shows that as of July 1, 2016, the actual size of the force, including first line supervisors and executives, is 2,000 and the starting pay is now up to $18.75 per hour, not very much for putting your life on the line day after day.

Many of the young officers I had tagged as potential felons became just that. The two that I stopped walking down the stairs to the locker room at Number 10 were both arrested for selling drugs. The two plainclothes officers, Starsky and Hutch, that I asked to be put back in uniform, beat a suspect to death with a heavy duty flashlight and were sentenced to long prisoner terms. Officer Richie, whom I asked to be taken off the street when I caught him kicking a suspect who was laying face down on the ground, later shot his wife and two year old daughter, and then killed himself.

Daily headlines in the *Detroit News and Free Press* warned the citizens of Detroit that there were nearly as many crooks on the police department as there were in their neighborhoods. One article called them street punks with badges. One of the S.T.R.E.S.S. officers involved in the shoot-out with the sheriff's deputies and three other DPD officers were later arrested, convicted, and sent to prison for guarding drug shipments for one of the biggest dope dealers in Detroit. Officers who were interviewed for the articles said department morale was at an all-time low.

That chief of police, the one who cussed me out, told me that I would never be promoted as long as he was there, and suggested that I resign, spent nine and a half of his ten year sentence in a federal penitentiary for stealing over two million dollars from funds the feds sent to Detroit to fight drug trafficking.

Detroit's Corporation Counsel became overwhelmed with lawsuits from officers and citizens and often the city settled rather than risk a costly court battle. Duty disabilities were handed out like candy and the city's coffers became a cash cow. Concessions to Detroit's powerful unions, the ones that actually ran the city, also took its toll on the city's finances, causing Detroit to become the largest city in the history of the United States to file for bankruptcy. The most costly concessions were large pension payments and health benefits. At the breakfast the retirees named seven retired deputy chiefs and chiefs who are getting a six figure retirement pension. That is ridiculous!

At the time I retired, an officer received two percent of his or her last salary for every year completed on the job, maxing out at thirty-five years and seventy percent. Currently, retiring officers start out at sixty-two percent and max out in just twelve years at eight-one percent.

A ruling by a federal judge now prohibits residency as a requirement for employment for law enforcement officers. This means that Detroit officers can now legally take the money they earned in Detroit and buy their homes, cars, food, clothing, furnishing, and whatever else they chose to purchase in the suburbs. Tax revenues also took a big hit in

Detroit. Officers now pay a non-resident income tax instead of the more costly resident income tax.

Folks like Vivian, George, Stanley, Dorothy, Nate, Walter, and a few others, worked hard for what they got and did not kiss ass or suck up to the bosses to get where they were. They were standouts and deserved every promotion they received. On the other hand, there were those who had their head stuck so far up the chief's behind that had he made a sudden stop, they would have suffocated.

Several of these new executives had worked for me either as a police officer or sergeant and I often had to read their report several times and overlook their poor spelling and rambling sentences before I could decipher what actually happened at the crime scene. When I returned to Detroit and saw these same officers wearing their oak leaves, silver eagles, gold bars, and spaghetti on their caps, the first thought to come to my mind was, "He made inspector, and she made commander? "You have got to be kidding me!"

On the personal side, George, Vivian, and I have not stopped communicating since I left the force. He and I talk at least three or four times a week and on NFL Sundays we talk from the first game to the last one. After Vivian's only relative in Arizona, her mother, passed away, she moved to Florida, about fifteen miles from me. She has cousins here in Florida and in Georgia. As far as the women who played a major role in my life are concerned, neither Lola nor Bette Jo remarried.

Lola and I have remained good friends over the years and I cannot say enough about the tremendous job she has done as a single mother in raising our daughters to be the outstanding young women they are today, and of whom we are both very proud. Tracey works as an executive assistant for a major corporation and has her own travel and consultant businesses on the side called Wanna Have Fun, LLC and Simple Logic Administrative Management/Consulting. Theresa has earned a

263

Bachelors and a Masters degree in International Studies from Georgetown University and NYU and through her organization called Blackbread she has created international cultural exchange programs for minorities to study abroad. Theresa speaks fluent Russian, Spanish and is able to hold conversations in several other languages. Currently, much of her time is being spent in Moscow and the Czech Republic. Tracey is passing her skills onto her daughter Ashley, who is also an agent in the travel business. Ashley's son Caine is just enjoying the life of an eight year old who is being spoiled rotten by his parents, grandparents, and great grandparents.

Renee got off drug and did marry. She has two children, and is also raising one of her sister's children. I have not seen her in over twenty years.

For the first twenty-five years after my separation and divorce I dated a number of women, but purposely did not allow any of the relationships to reach the one-year mark. I always found a reason to bring it to an end or gave them a reason to end it. Why, I cannot give you a rational answer.

Then I met Gertha. When Gertha and I were nearing the end our eleventh month of dating, the thought of ending the relationship never crossed my mind. In fact, I was determined as ever to complete that one-year mark. Why the change in attitude? All I will say is that it was due to that second epiphany I mentioned earlier. The first epiphany was when my dad came to get my mother at the hospital. The second one told me not to let Gertha go and I didn't.

After a ten year courtship that was frequently interrupted by my refusal to admit what I had, and me, with my sixty-six-year old ass, still trying to get in just one more romance, I finally came to my senses, stopped fighting the inevitable, and we jumped the broom. I believe that had it not been for Gertha's strong belief in God, and the great times and travels we had whenever we were together, she would have dropped my ass after the third or fourth year. I am very glad she didn't.

Gertha has four children, twelve grandchildren, and four great-grands. It has now been seven years of marriage plus the ten year courtship, and we are growing stronger each and every year, and our two families have merged into one.

On the law enforcement side, many of my friends were relieved when I left the job but were also saddened because I did not accomplish my goal of commanding my own precinct and wearing that spaghetti on my hat. But all was not lost. I did what I said I was going to do and I fulfilled my childhood dream. I became a police officer. I just happened to join the wrong department.

They say everything happens for a reason. My embarrassing and humiliating departure may have been the best thing that ever happened to me. After leaving the force, I did what all of us say we are going to do once we retire. I wrote a book, and I went on a travel binge making stops in forty-nine states. There is one state I have not visited yet because I'm afraid I may run into Sarah Palin and ruin the trip. I traveled all across Europe, stopping in London, Paris, Rome, Germany, Switzerland, and Amsterdam. I walked through the Coliseum and sat in the sanctuary at the Vatican under the window where the Pope gives his weekly address.

In the Middle East I visited the birthplace of Jesus and the room where the Last Supper was held. I sailed down the Nile, dipped my foot in the River Jordan, fished in the Suez Canal, floated in the Dead Sea, and rode a camel around the Pyramids. Let's not forget Mexico, Cuba, Puerto Rico, and over a dozen Caribbean Islands. I met and took pictures with over thirty movie stars, professional athletes, and three former U S presidents. I have appeared in television commercials, sitcoms, and feature films as an extra. However, don't blink or you may miss me. I also ran a marathon. And as a family oriented man, I made it a point to

265

visit every relative I possibly could from New York to Los Angeles, and those in between. My last three cars have a combined total of 650,000 miles.

Giddy up Horsey!

The best job that I ever had in my entire life, bar none, was in 2002 when I became a member of the late Janet Reno's executive staff. The former United States Attorney General under President Clinton was running for governor of Florida. Those of you who follow Florida politics know that the so called I-4 Corridor is the key to winning any statewide or national election. So goes the I-4 Corridor, so goes Florida. My official job title was "Western I-4 Corridor Regional Field Coordinator."

I was in charge of eleven counties. My job was to set up and coordinate all of her appearances on the Westside of the I-4 corridor. I was in charge of hundreds of volunteers. It was here that I found out up close and personal just how dirty politics can really be as we have just witnessed in the 2016 presidential race. I watched as Florida's Republican and Democratic parties conspired to deny Janet the nomination. She was a fantastic person, and it was hard to watch what was taking place. It was like watching Frank and President Obama all over again.

I un-retired a half dozen times over the years. My final job was that of emergency management coordinator at Bethune-Cookman University where I began turning their entire safety program around in just a few short months, updating their current safety and emergency notification procedures and introduced a few of my own. All buildings were assigned a captain and co-captain whose responsibility was to be accountable for locating all personnel in cases of an evacuation. Due to all of the hurricanes in Florida, a safe room with no windows was established in each building.

There were only two negatives that had a lasting impact on my life after leaving the force. The first was my bogus arrest on two felony charges in Orlando in 1994 and being escorted from my apartment building in handcuffs with all of my neighbors watching. It was the *ultimate humiliation* of my life, even more than my suspension. This was the first and only time in my *entire life* that I honestly wanted to kill another human being outside the line of duty. I wrote a Made-for-Television movie about the arrest. It is called *Love Thy Neighbor*. The script is still sitting in my file cabinet. I could not finish it.

The second negative was the betrayal and tossing under the bus by Jerry L. Demmings, a friend of twenty years, who after seeing what I had done during the Reno campaign came to me and asked for my help in making him the first black sheriff in the history of Orange County, Florida. I did just that. I started by introducing him and his candidacy to the ninety-five guests at my 65th birthday party, and began recruiting volunteers right then and there. I had his back from day one. By the end of the campaign I was working sixty hours a week and often thirteen days in a row. From Monday through Friday I was in the office, out collecting, processing and depositing thousands of dollars in campaign contributions, coordinating and attending fundraiser all across the county, and on Saturdays we spent the day going door to door passing out flyers.

After the endorsement from his predecessor, who had been sheriff the past twenty years, and his election day victory, Sheriff Demmings went from being a law enforcement officer to a politician with a badge and now had no further use for me or my services. He failed to recognize me at his acceptance speech despite the fact that I was thirty feet away, he left me off the invitation list for his swearing in ceremony, and he rewarded several other members of our executive committee with jobs in the Orange County Sheriff's Department with salaries ranging from $78,000- $122,000. He said that he was not angry with me, that I had done nothing wrong, and that job offer was still forth coming. However, when I asked to meet with him to discuss these and other matters, he informed by telephone that his schedule was too busy to meet with me.

His betrayal was followed with an embarrassing, degrading and "slap in the face" job offer after my twelve month long dedicated and tireless effort to get him elected. My resume' includes an Associate's Degree, Bachelor's Degree, high school biology teacher, executive lieutenant on the nation's fifth largest police department, a juvenile probation officer, and an emergency management coordinator for a major university. Despite these accomplishments, and just before his shoo in reelection four years later, Jerry notified my by telephone that if I still wanted to work for the Orange County Sheriff's Department, he had openings for school crossing guards. Enough said.

For the past twenty years I have been helping Dr. Angela Adams to conduct health summits for Black, Haitian, Caribbean and Hispanic men in my five county area. I am a twenty-two year prostate cancer survivor. Although the gesture is symbolic, much like an honorary degree, as a show of appreciation for my health summit efforts, the mayor declared August 11, 2009 as James Edward Crawford day in the City of Orlando. The president of the city council presented me with a formal Proclamation; Congresswoman Corrine Brown's chief of staff presented me with a United States Congressional Commendation, and the godson of civil rights activist Rosa Parks, presented me with the prestigious Rosa Parks Community Service Award and a huge photograph of the former civil rights leader. Only a few have been given out.

Me & Dr. Angela Adams – Founder & CEO
Orlando's Annual Black Men's Health Summit

269

My Prospective

Despite what happened to me personally, and what is going on today with all of the police shootings of unarmed black men, I hold no ill will against police officers as a whole, just those who ruin it for the rest of us with their racism and bullying and with the juries who let them go scot free. That is why I often engage in conversations with officers whenever I can, why I take a picture alongside a police car when I visit major cities, and that is why my eyes still light up when I see police action taking place. It is still in my blood. I left being a cop, but it has never left me. Like the caption says, "Once a Cop, Always a Cop.

I'm not sure if the cause of my shattered dream was resolved or not. Was it my fault, the fault of the Detroit Police Department, my colleagues, superiors and subordinates, or was it just a continuous series of errors in judgment on my part combined with a countless number of unfortunate situations and circumstances? Even the psychiatrists could not reach an agreement on this one.

I am of the opinion that life is meant to be lived and enjoyed. I have tried to do that ever since I was a child. One cannot spend their life trying to please and do that which is best for others just to gain their love, respect, support, approval, or in my case a promotion. You owe it to yourself to do that which is best for you, your family, and your way of thinking, while at the same time not being rude or dismissive of the opinions of others. No matter how a person chooses to handle a situation there will always be those who will disagree with, and will be critical of their decision and/or methodology. This is what makes us individuals.

After it is all said and done, I am happy where I am in life, and it does not owe me a thing. I've been there and done that. No regrets.

Gertha and me – July 2016

My daughters Tracey and Theresa

My granddaughter Ashley and me

My great-grandson Caine

My good buddy George

My BFF – Vivian

Folks I Bumped Into Along the Way

Office Christmas party in New York City.
My daughter worked for him

With Vice President Al Gore
Florida Democrataic Convention

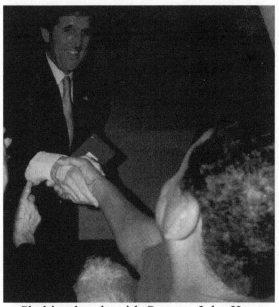

Shaking hands with Senator John Kerry
At Florida Democratic Covention

With Janet Reno at my 60th birthday party

With Martin Sheen at Janet Reno rally

With Adams Sandler in the Movie
Water Boy

With Sidney Poitier while shooting a made for television movie *Separate but Equal*

With Bette Midler in commercial for the New York Lottery

With Cuba Gooding Jr. while shooting
the movie - *Instinct*

With comedian Dick Gregory at African American
Men's Health Summit in Orlando

279

With Dan Aykroyd and Jamie Lee Curtis
while shooting the Movie - *My Girl*

Jamie Lee and me – *My Girl*

With Macaulay Culkin – *My Girl*

With John Stamos in a Beach Boys video
Hot Fun in the Summer Time

281

With Hulk Hogan in a television Series
Thunder in Paradise

Jimmy Crawford as the Ninja
Thunder in Paradise

With Henry Winkler (the Fonz) in the
movie – *Water Boy*

With Lawrence Taylor in the Movie
Water Boy

283

With Roy Scheider, of Jaws fame in made for TV
movie – *Someone Has to Shoot the Picture*

With Suzanne Somers in the television show
Step by Step

With Ossie Davis at Zora Neal Hurston Festival
in Eatonville, Florida

With Wesley Snipes in the movie
Passenger 57

285

With golfer Arnold Palmer at Fundraiser in Orlando

With Barry Sanders at a Tampa Bay Bucs vs. Detroit
Lions game in Tampa, Florida

With Shaquille O'Neal at a fundraiser in Orlando

Muhammad Ali's autograph
No Camera Available

From the television series *Swamp Thing*
(I was killed in the opening scene – Damn!)

With the Buffalo Soldiers in Tampa, Florida

Made in the USA
Lexington, KY
06 April 2017